Tales from the Foxes' Den
2015 Anthology

A Collection of Short Stories

by the

Writers of

FoxTale Book Shoppe

Copyright © 2015 Beth Hermes

All rights reserved.

ISBN-10: 151938047X
ISBN-13:978-1519380470

DEDICATION

This book is dedicated to the dreams and efforts of the Writers of FoxTale Book Shoppe's workshops and classes.

These are their stories...

ACKNOWLEDGMENTS

In addition to the exceptional work of the writers whose stories are contained within these pages, this book would not be possible without the participation of the inspired individuals who participated in the 8-week writing workshops, 12-week creativity workshops, 3-hour Saturday Boot Camps, and Quarterly Saturday Critiques, as well as the All-Night Writers who camp out at the shop each November for a full night of creating new stories.

Heartfelt thanks to the Foxes of FoxTale Book Shoppe – Karen Schwettmann, Jackie Tanase, and Ellen Ward – for providing the den where we can be inspired by one another. And to Gary Parkes and Valerie Hudgins, whose tireless efforts in publicizing our classes, book launches, Emerging Author events, and more, allow new writers to find us and hone their craft.

The Foxes: Karen, Ellen & Jackie

CONTRIBUTING WRITERS

Linda Fowler Coe	Cheryl Taylor
Crystal Wheeler	Maureen Krivo
Debi Barrington Merchant	Debra Mihalic Staples
Maxene D. Raices	Betsy Scott
Cindy DuGan	Victoria Lynne Yoder
Gretchen K. Corbijn	Dawn T. Walker
Terri Slone	Roger Brooks Wilson, Sr.
Tina Burns	Carolynn Mann
Debbie House	Julie Couse
Elise Noelle	

Tales From The Foxes' Den 2015 – An Introduction

When visitors step through the doors of FoxTale Book Shoppe for the very first time, they see the books, they admire the décor, (they often ask for the restroom), and sometimes they stop and listen to the stories being shared among those sitting at the table in between the bookshelves.

The stories are inspired, amazing, well-crafted... and usually written in less than three minutes by members of one of the many Writing Classes and Workshops that take place at FoxTale.

One of the most common laments among these writers (note: they are not *aspiring* writers – they are WRITERS) was that they were not published, and they weren't sure their wonderful stories would ever find an audience outside of the classes.

In 2014, we put forth a challenge to the FoxTale Writers: take at least one class before October, write and edit your best work (2,500 words or less), and turn in that piece to be published in an Anthology that will be offered as a special publication at FoxTale Book Shoppe.

We had 12 writers that first year. This year, we have 19, and the stories they share are as unique and wonderful as the writers themselves.

Writers have to start somewhere, and for most of us, that "somewhere" is in a private space in our homes or in a journal or on a computer; at the end of our "writing session," we turn out the lights, we close the journal, we save (or not) the work to our hard drive, and we tell ourselves that is enough.

Until it is not.

So we take a class, and we share our work with our fellow writers around the table, and we laugh and we go home and we say that it is enough.

Until it is not.

Writers, like all artists, need something to propel them to finish what they start, and that finish includes finding an audience who will add their stories to bookshelves, night stands, coffee tables, and recommended reading lists, to enjoy again and again as part of a book.

Linda, Crystal, Debi, Maxene, Cindy, Gretchen, Terri, Tina, Debbie, Elise, Cheryl, Maureen, Debra, Betsy, Victoria, Dawn, Roger, Carolynn, and Julie took a huge step forward in allowing their work to be published (*PUBLISHED!*) in this Anthology. And that is enough, for now...

Until it is not – and we do this again next year!

We all thank you for purchasing this Second Annual Anthology: Tales From The Foxes's Den 2015, and we hope you enjoy the stories within these pages.

-Beth Hermes
Author & Writing Coach

LINDA FOWLER COE

Linda's first attempt at writing was a play, entitled, "Bells On Their Toes." She was in the 9th grade, and the play was performed at the high school in her hometown.

Her love of writing continued, and she graduated from the University of South Alabama with a degree in English, then spent the next three decades as a Delta Airlines flight attendant and supervisor of In-flight services, before retiring in 2001.

Linda began taking writing classes in 2013, and has developed a gift for writing memoir and fantasy.

In addition to writing, Linda enjoys gardening, cooking, and fishing.

She lives in Marietta, Georgia.

Lavender and Lye

If you've never stepped off the porch early in the morning into a pile of chicken "doo doo," you've never lived in the country. Of course, you were barefoot and the squishy, wet stuff was still cool due to the night air. You scraped sand from the yard and rubbed it between your toes and all over your foot to remove the disgusting mess. Carefully, you made your way through these nasty drippings to the well for a dipper of cold, crisp water. Then you had the joy of being chased by a flock of screeching, pecking, wing-flapping chickens as you kicked up dust running for the out-house. When you left, the fear of confronting the meanest bantam rooster God ever made loomed over you! My sister and I went together 'cause Ma and Pa had a two-holer and we were of afraid of going by ourselves, due to those loud, crazy chickens!
    Once we arrived safely back to the kitchen, we were in for a treat of hot biscuits, red-eye gravy, fresh eggs, pancakes, home-made butter, bacon, and a choice of jelly, preserves, or cane syrup! Thinking about those days now, I wonder if anyone ever appreciated how early Aunt Sissy hd to get up to prepare all that food on an old wood-burning stove.

    My sister and I frequently spent time during the summer with my grandma, grandpa and Aunt Sissy. We always had fun, except for the chores! After breakfast it was mine and my sister's job to sweep and rake the big dirt yard. First we swept all the trash, acorns and chicken droppings with straw brooms all the way across Ma and Pa's big dirt yard to the fence or the road. Next we had to rake the yard and make perfectly even lines in the freshly swept dirt. The lines had to be neat and straight so that passers-by would know the chores were being done, and not speak of our family as a "lazy bunch." Funny that nobody ever told the chickens not to poop or scratch!

Once we finished all our chores, we excitedly ran to the back porch, poured a pan of water, scrubbed our hands and arms, and then dried them on the aprons we seemed doomed to wear. We sat on the back porch steps anticipating our mid-morning treat. Finally Sissy brought each of us a cold biscuit wrapped in waxed paper. We turned our large, crusty biscuit on its side and delicately pushed a finger into it and made a hole all the way until just past the center. Sissy slowly filled the holes with thick, homemade cane syrup. No cookie has ever tasted that good!

Once our chores were done we were free to play, and play we did! We played hop scotch, doodle bug, jump rope, jacks, pick-up sticks, marbles, yo-yo, all kinds of card games, and made the greatest mud pies in the world! I was the yo-yo champ of my class. I could "walk the dog," "go around the world," and "see-saw" better than anybody! I also loved cat eye marbles, and won quite a collection in my day.

Pa was an expert at making pea shooters and sling shots. When the cousins came to visit he would make each of us one. Our mamas were very displeased with him, but he just laughed. We only shot at bottles and paper targets until they went back to quilting and gossiping. Free at last, we went romping through the woods and spent many hours waging war with dried peas and china berries.

We all loved Pa so much! He had a head full of thick white hair, a bulbous red nose and eyes that were bright with laughter. He stood about six feet two inches tall and seemed to tower over us. He always wore a long-sleeved white shirt with either khaki pants and suspenders, or overalls. He never ventured anywhere without one of his homemade canes. Pa told all of us cousins scary stories, gave us maps to find buried treasures, and whittled wooden toys for us. He was our hero and we followed him everywhere he went, except the outhouse!

One afternoon, he gathered us into a huddle and whispered that we were going on an adventure. He mysteriously beckoned that we quietly follow him. The seven of us did not mutter a sound as we trailed after Pa through the front yard, across the dirt road, and into the pasture toward the tree line. Pa suddenly stopped and signaled that we could relax now that we were out of sight and sound of the bickering women. We sat down in the pasture by the trees as Pa explained our new adventure. We were so excited! We were to look at trees, saplings, bushes and underbrush for a special twig. The twig must have a "Y" shape at one end and be about three feet in total length. As we located our twigs, Pa would approve the best ones and use his ever-present pocket knife to cut it off at just the right place. Once the twigs were collected, with a mischievous look in his eyes he yelled, "Let's go dowsing!" Needless to say, we did not know what dowsing meant, but it sounded exciting! We all went walking in the pasture until we finally stopped for Pa to illustrate the procedure of finding underground water. Holding our twigs by the legs of the "Y," we walked with arms straight out. Pa told us that if suddenly our twig turned down toward the ground, there was water underneath that spot. We found enough water that afternoon to float a ship!

Ma was a tiny woman with a sour disposition, who never laughed nor smiled. Her long, thin hair had never been cut and was always slicked back into a bun on the back of her head. She wore stockings that she pulled up and over her calves, then rolled them down a couple of times, twisted them into a knot she tucked underneath the roll to hold them up. He shoes were ugly lace-ups with metal rings through which she threaded the shoe laces.

All day you could find her sitting in her rocking chair with a straght-backed chair beside her. On the seat of this chair she kept snuff, a spit cup, a wad of Juicy Fruit chewing gum, and a new pack for when the "flavor" was gone from the wad in her mouth. She never offered us one piece! Much of the time she took to her "sick bed." We scattered out into the yard when she did, 'cause we knew she was going to grab one of us to rub her boney feet and toes with her liniment stuff. It assaulted your nose and the awful odor hung around on your hands all day!

Ma's personality changed on quilting day. Three or four of her friends arrived wearing their bonnets and, of course, their prettiest aprons. One brought fresh peaches, another boiled peanuts, another homemade cookies. And there was the ever-present pitcher of sweet tea. The quilting frame was lowered from the ceiling and the ladies took their places with needles and thread to begin work on their latest work of art. Every quilt I saw was beautiful. I now have three of these quilts, which I treasure.

Aunt Sissy was fun! She made her own "drawers" out of white flour sacks. She used the "flowered" flour sacks for making her aprons and bonnets. I don't remember ever seeing her without an apron tied around her waist, except on Sunday afternoons. She took us with her in the mornings to gather eggs from beneath the hens. I was never successful in pulling an egg from the nest, 'cause I was afraid a hen would peck me! After gathering the eggs, we tagged along with her to milk the cows, Molly and Elsie. My sister held the bucket under the cow's udders while Sissy pulled on each one with perfect rhythm. I can still hear the sound of the milk hitting the bucket. We always had fresh milk and butter. I learned to churn milk at an early age. After churning the milk for as long as it takes Christmas to come, Sissy skimmed the cream off the top, made butter from it, and spread it to harden in small wooden molds. Then she placed it into the ice box to harden for breakfast the next morning.

Aunt Sissy also taught us how to catch a chicken and wring its neck. The chicken hopped and flopped around until it was dead. Then she chopped off its head, tied heavy twine around its feet and hung it up on a hook attached to the eave of the back porch roof. After a few minutes, she took it down and dipped it into a pot of boiling water to soften the skin so the feathers could be easily plucked. After plucking, she hung the chicken back up, lit a long kitchen match and singed the leftover down feathers. Preparing a chicken for cooking was a gruesome process, but it was as common back then as bringing chicken home from the supermarket is now.

    Sissy cleaned our clothes with lye soap and boiling water in a big black wash pot in the back yard. She used a bit wooden paddle to stir them around in the hot water until they were clean. Then she rinsed them in well water, squeezed them out and hung them on the clothesline to dry. I can close my eyes and feel the warm breeze that gently danced with the sheets, causing them to sway in unison to the movement of that sweet wind. Our clothes always smelled as clean and fresh as sunshine on a spring morning.

    One of the fondest memories I have of Sissy is her garden. She never failed to let us help plant a huge garden of her favorite flowers called zinnias. When they grew tall and bloomed, we cut them and scattered the colors of the rainbow throughout the whole house in Mason jars filled with water. They brought beauty to the old house that would have made Miss Scarlett proud!

    The times we really looked forward to were Sunday afteronnons when Sissy's boyfriend, Wilbur, came to call on her. She took a bath, sprinkled herself with lavender scented powder, and put on her favorite Sears and Roebuck dress. Then she pulledon pink or white socks with a frilly lace top and slipped her small feet into a pair of beige low-heeled pumps she had also ordered from a catalogue. Wilbur was always right on time! They sat on the front porch in rocking chairs, talked for a while and then went for a ride in his shiny green truck. I was too young to know what the phrase "making out" meant, but as I got older I wondered if that was what they did on those truck rides! He was truly the love of her life.

    After Ma and Pa died, my aunt and uncle from a small town near Mobile, Alabama, took Sissy to live with them. Although she was well taken care of, everything there was foreign to her. She no longer had her own home, her chickens, her zinnias, her yard, or her own routine. Wilbur married a younger woman, but out of love and kindness nobody ever told her. Sissy died a few years later, at the age of sixty-two. I can still see her in the garden cutting zinnias, wearing her colorful apron and bonnet.

CRYSTAL WHEELER

Crystal has always wanted to write, but never felt like she had anything to say. Her first attempt was "a horrible song, when I was 13. The next piece I wrote was from a writing prompt that began, 'The hallway was silent.' My story ended with my boyfriend handing me dog poop. Go figure!"

She began taking classes 3 ½ years ago, and has taken "pretty much every one they offer" since then. Her unique perspective makes Crystal a natural for her favorite style of writing: Humor!

After attending the University of Kentucky, Crystal has spent the last 37 years in radio and television as an audio engineer. She now pursues writing when not at her full-time jobs, and hopes to volunteer with the Alzheimer's Association, in honor of her Mom.

Crystal lives in Acworth, Georgia, with her Mom (she has Alzheimer's... so each day is brand new!), her boyfriend of nine years, Mark, two dogs (Murphy Brown and Roscoe – aka "loose cannon"), and a 20-pound cat (don't judge!) named Rocko.

Adventures with the Co-Dependents

My best friend, Mindy, had been attending Co-Dependents Anonymous. I wanted to go – I wanted in – surely I was co-dependent and fucked up enough to belong. "Please", I begged (not sure why I felt the need to have her blessing – I guess I was just that Co-Dependent! Ha...I told you!) She agreed that I could meet her at the meeting (oh, joy!!) but gave strict instructions not to sit with her. I was not surprised by this request as we had gone through the same thing when I mentioned attending the same church. She told me "I don't mind if you go...but don't sit with me. I'll feel smothered!" If you are wondering at this point, are we still friends? We are not!

    The meeting was on a Monday night at a huge church. There was some kind of meeting within a meeting formatics and then we broke into smaller groups. The smaller groups were held in various rooms around the church. I knew that I would have to seek out a room that my friend was not in... so, I just went the opposite way down the hallway. There were about eight or nine people in each group. A girl, let's just say her name was Kelly, because it was, seemed to know everyone in our group and seemingly every other group as well. She was very loud and kept asking people where they were going for dinner. She really didn't seem concerned about where I wanted to go or the fact that she was talking across me and not including me in any of the conversation.

Eventually, the group came to order and people started to "check in" – which basically consisted of going around the room, introducing yourself by first name only, and expressing how you were feeling – physically, emotionally and spiritually. I don't really remember my "check in" that night…but I do remember my never-to-be-good-friend Kelly's. It was very memorable because everything she said was preceded by air quotes and followed by the same. For instance, when she expressed feeling thirsty as her physical condition – she was waving those quoting fingers in the air. After the meeting, there was a lot of hugging, not including me – but around me. Oh, there were a few folks who welcomed me – but then they all headed out to this elusive dinner – without me – I left that meeting determined to crack the co-dependent code – to fit in and if I had to – to be as fucking sick as this bunch. I had to get in to the group. It is kind of like how I currently feel about the Mormon Temple – I am going to get in there one day.

    The next few meetings were not very eventful. I may have started to fit in a little – not a lot – but just a little. I was learning the ins and outs of sharing. There was the lady who would always lean all the way over and touch her ankles when she started to share. There was Nancy Johnson – who no matter how many times she was told that no one used their last names in the meetings – she insisted on giving hers every time. There was the chick with red hair that would take her watch off and stare at it while people were sharing as if she were the official time keeper. When she did this when I was sharing – it just forced me to talk much slower and throw a bunch of sick shit into the mix. I had plenty of it. There was the British woman who hosted a radio show – I just wanted to hear about her show – of course, she would not talk about that…and last but not least, my air quote friend, Kelly, who never got tired of flailing those arms about. She must have been exhausted after a meeting. I know I was after watching her.

    I started to permeate this co-dependent culture – even got invited to dinner. I started to get familiar with the lingo. For example, when Barbara (another co-dependent) went to the shoe store and explained to the manager that the pumps that she was returning were cutting off her third chakra and if he didn't understand that – it was "his stuff" and not hers and apparently he was spiritually bankrupt and not in touch with his inner child. Apparently Doris (also a good co-dependent) was not able to hold a job because she could not connect with employers emotionally.

There were so many terms to learn...it was very overwhelming. Apparently everyone, at least this group of folks, is a mess!

Eventually the dinners started to lead to more...much more. Again, I was starting to be excluded. I was not invited to the after dinner affairs. Apparently, the meetings and dinners were no longer enough for the inner circle – they had to have more. The few, about ten in all, would take turns going to each others homes to spend the night. They would all sleep in the floor and anytime during the night if someone had any "feelings" come up...they were allowed to wake the others and talk about it...or process. This just sounded like something that would really piss me off if I was trying to sleep.

My friend, Mindy, who was included in the co-dependency inner-circle, would share stories with me about all of their emotional "connections" that were being achieved. She was starting to even use air quotes. Thanks, Kelly! I started to lose total interest...but then one day, something happened that intrigued me. She was talking about one night when around 4 am Daniel (I believe he was the only male in the inner circle) woke them up to tell them he had an erection. In my mind, I was nodding and thinking...now, we are getting somewhere! She went on and on about how his erection was a result of his chakra's aligning and how comfortable he was being in the group and being the only male. All I was hearing at this point was some kind of white noise. Then she said they all went back to sleep.

That's it?!?!? I screamed internally...WHAT?!?! That is all that happened?!?!

Needless to say, I never went back. I had gone deep enough, so to speak!

Brown Panties: A Love Story

First of all, let me reassure that the title of this story does not mean that I am bragging or that it is in any way a love story. I just think with the colon...and A Love Story...that my story will have a better chance of one day becoming a Lifetime movie...starring Ms. Ashley Judd.

Maybe I should brag because I feel certain that most of the females I know would not own up to the fact that they own brown panties. I honestly can't say that anyone really owns brown panties – with the exception of myself...and if anyone actually owns them...would they wear them?

Well, my story begins on a Saturday in April. My Dad & I went to Publix to pick up some groceries. It is very clear to all that know me that I am an impulse buyer - no shopping list for me – which usually means that I will have a cart full of stuff that I don't need and absolutely nothing that I needed from the store that prompted the trip. In other words, no items were purchased that would have been on this thing referred to as "a list." You may wonder what my point is...don't worry...I am used to it! The point is that my Dad finished shopping much earlier than I did...yes, he had a list...and he was waiting outside for me.

It was a sunny day and Daddy was standing outside the van. This apparently did not agree with some of his meds because when we got home...he collapsed in the garage. He was okay...but did sprain his ankle.

My Mom liked to send my Dad to the grocery store every day...not for a huge trip...but to pick up just a couple of things she felt we needed.

The day that my Dad collapsed – I knew that Mom was going to send me back to the store...so I decided to do a preemptive strike. I was going to work the NBA playoffs the next day...and we had three games back to back. I didn't want to have to make a trip to the store on Sunday morning...so, I asked the proverbial question – "do you need anything else from the store?" I also proclaimed that I was not – under any circumstances going to the story next day. Well, my preemptive strike didn't actually work out (do they ever?) Mom said she didn't need anything on Saturday night – but Sunday morning was a different story.

I got up Sunday morning. I worked out – stop laughing – I did...it was a different time. Then I took a shower and went downstairs to eat some breakfast... I had left just enough time before I had to leave for work. Well, let's just say that breakfast didn't happen...because it didn't. As soon as I got to the bottom of the steps, Mom told me she needed me to go to the store. Of course, I became irate! I didn't want to go to the store and was sure that I had no time...but my Mom was insisting. She didn't drive and Daddy was down for the count, so, guilt got the best of me and I went to the damn store! The list was small – hamburger buns and ice cream! All necessary items!

Begrudgingly – I went to the store. I came home in a huff. I brought the groceries in the house and was putting them away – when my Mother walked in and said "your ass is hanging out of your jeans!"

What?!?!?

She said, "Your ass is hanging out of your jeans!"

Okay – I was not sure what that meant – but, I felt of my ass and yes, it indeed, was hanging out! I knew the jeans that I was wearing had had a hole near the seam – but I didn't realize that somewhere between my house and Publix that the seam had split right down the middle.

Now, here comes the brown panties part of this tale...get it, panties...tail...anyway...

That is what I was wearing...brown panties underneath my entire ass hanging out pair of jeans. That is probably what most of the folks were looking at as I strolled through Publix – my brown panty covered ass.

Most people would be horrified by this event. I guess that I was a little shaken up by all of this – but if I am honest – my hope is that all of the folks who witnessed this spectacle just thought I had a really good tan...on my ass!!!!

Hot Or Homeless.com

There seems to be a dating site that would or should at least, appeal to every interest or perhaps any fetish – even some unmentionable quirks that would be hard to classify.

I should be totally upfront and disclose that I have used a couple of these dating sites (or more!). I even met my boyfriend Mark on a dating website. I should also disclose that the website I met Mark on did not charge a fee. This truly proves that you do get exactly what you pay for.

I actually never paid for any matchmaking websites.

Maybe some really savvy advertising firm should snag me as a spokesperson for paid websites. I could be the "don't be like me" photo. Always the before – never the after…story of my life!

My first experience with this new social world was with a dating site for people with Psoriasis. I met the entrance requirement, so, I thought – what the hell!! I posted a pic and filled out the questionnaire. I did this pretty late at night – when everything seems like a much better idea than it ever would by the light of day.

The next day – not the first thing – I was not completely desperate – maybe a 6 on a scale of 1 to 10 on the desperation scale…oh, shit, who am I kidding…probably I was more like a 9.99 on that scale (10 being the most desperate!)…I did check to see if anyone wanted to connect – and low and behold…I had a "taker"…so to speak.

Interestingly enough, I do not remember anything about this "taker" with the exception of what he "wanted" in a relationship. His basic needs were very simple…he was looking for sex and maybe dating. Wow! Talk about cutting to the chase – I guess there was no need to mince words or waste time. Now the choice was up to me – could I provide this gentleman's basic needs and did I want to provide those? I knew one thing for sure: if I met up with "Mr. Right Now" – I damn sure better have dinner first because there may be no "dating" involved. Maybe his plan was to split a can of soup after sex. I have had worse in my time around the block – note I said "time" not "times" and block is singular as well!

I somehow was able to resist temptation and not respond to this interested party. Try to shake that surprised look off of your face please!!

My next venture into the cyber dating world was on a website that was dedicated to my particular political party. Without saying too much...let me just share that Fox News is not part of my channel guide. I bet you are surprised at that one!

On this website, there were no takers. What the hell? I may have wanted it too much!

Another dating site that caters to women who are - let's just say – because we are – weight challenged and the men who love them – is called Big Beautiful Women. I certainly fit 2 of those categories – I would really rather not talk about which ones apply.

A gentleman contacted me. He was "hair challenged" with a really wide part and weighed about 80 pounds. I never met with him in person – but after a couple of phone conversations – I realized that he was a very strong Baptist Republican...and anyone who really knows me could tell you that these are two traits that I am not seeking in a mate. No offense meant to any Baptist Republican friends who may be reading this.

My next venture into cyber dating and hopefully my last – was on a website that some friends of mine had helped start – although I am pretty sure that up to this moment – they were probably unaware that I was introduced to Mark on their website. They should not worry – I am not filing suit against them yet – we are only 9 years into our relationship – you have to give these things time – not the lawsuit, although I am sure that would take time as well – relationships take time – you know, to see where they are going.

When I signed up on this website, there was an option to pay, which, I, of course, ignored. There were a few "takers" – again, so to speak – on this website – none that I was interested in – but then, I was contacted by Mark. He had beautiful blue eyes and facial hair – which apparently was about all it took for me to become interested. We talked on the phone a few times before we set up our mysterious in person meeting – I am not sure why I have declared this meeting as mysterious – it happened in the parking lot at a Chick Fil A in Hiram, GA. That seems to be a hot spot for young singles to meet. Well, maybe not young – at least in our case, but singles anyway.

Long story short – nine years later – we are still together – take that all you people who paid for dating websites and then it didn't work out. Wait, maybe I should take that back!!

Anyway, let's fast forward to now and to my amazing new business idea. The patent may or may not be pending on this idea – so, please don't yield to temptation to try to cash in – you know who you are.

Since I have always been attracted to the long haired, and of course, the bearded – I have come up with an idea for a new dating site – that will appeal to ladies like me (and maybe some fellas – we will not discriminate!). It would seem that for no particular reason, a large number of men, that I would consider "hot" are also sometimes homeless as well. That might be a twofer for me and perhaps some others. This seems to be a totally untapped market – which could be a plus for me – but now, I have decided to stop trying to keep all the "hot" and often "homeless" gents for myself. I am going to expose this dating sector to the public.

My new venture is called Hot or Homeless.com. There will be no charge for this service to either party.

Okay, maybe I have not thought planned this endeavor out very well. Maybe I should not make all these "hotties" available via the web.

Maybe I should not quit my day job.

Whoa! That was close!

DEBI BARRINGTON MERCHANT

Debi says she caught the bug to write after reading <u>Gone With the Wind,</u> and penned her first "book" entitled, "All's Well That Ends Well," when she was just 13 years old. She kept the handwritten manuscript (an author *never* discards her work!)

She graduated from high school (and hopes to go to college, "when I grow up!"), then spent more than 34 years in civilian service with the U.S. Government, before retiring in 2008.

In 2007, Debi completed and published a work of creative non-fiction, entitled <u>Dancing In the Garage</u>, which details her faith journey. In addition to this genre, she is trying her hand at Modern Southern Gothic fiction.

Her love of writing has her writing two books at the moment – a novel, and a non-fiction devotional book. She also may attempt to write a children's book. "I bought 10 ISBN numbers... I plan to use them all!" she says.

Debi is married to Matthew Merchant. She has three grown kids and three grandchildren.

Musings of the Deacon's Daughter

I am "the deacon's daughter", and I must say that at age 62 I'm very proud of that distinction – although that has not always been the case. No, there were times when I was told that I couldn't do this or that because "you're the deacon's daughter", and I thought it was the biggest curse ever!

It was the spring of 1971, and I was a senior in high school. I was also the church pianist. The "preacher's daughter" was one of my best friends and was the organist at our church. She was a junior, but was dating a senior. I won't bore you with all the details, but let's just say that the prom fell on the last night of revival week at our church. Did I mention that I was a senior? It was my **senior prom**. Long story short, the "preacher's daughter" went to the prom (did I mention that she was a JUNIOR?), and the "deacon's daughter" went to revival and played the piano. I know, I know - it's been 44 years – let it go, Debi, let it go.

"I'm American by birth, and Southern by the grace of God". I'm not sure where that quote originated, but I first heard it from my daddy... a YANKEE! Yep, he was born in the state of Ohio, and the last time I looked it was above the Mason/Dixon Line. So Daddy was a "naturalized" Southerner. The family joke is that at age two he talked his folks into moving to Pensacola, FL, so he could grow up in the South – "by the grace of God".

Since Daddy, Jerry Creighton Barrington, was named for his great-grandfather, Jeroboam Creighton, who served in the Union Army, he was given the diary that Jeroboam wrote during the Civil War.

It is an awesome experience to read that diary,

especially now that I live in the Atlanta area because he fought in the battles of Kennesaw Mountain and Atlanta! The diary made the history books come alive for me since it was written by my own flesh and blood!

One of my favorite childhood memories is our annual kite flying adventure. Neither of us were any good at flying kites, but each March Daddy and I would head out to buy the perfect kite. We'd come home, create the perfect tail using an old sheet, hooking up all the string carefully weaving it just so, and then we'd head outside with our masterpiece that we both KNEW was the best kite EVER! We'd run like wild people through the yard with the kite trailing behind us. It would get some lift and begin to ascend into the heavens, and then after about two seconds it would promptly crash into a million pieces. We'd look at each other like two scientists in a lab, scratch our heads, pick up all the pieces, and head back into the house to repair the kite, so that we could start all over again. Ah, those were the days.

Daddy and I loved to disagree on a number of things just for the heck of it, arguing profusely about any and everything – especially politics and religion (specifically our differing interpretations of the Scripture). We locked horns and butted heads for as long as I can remember, but through it all, our love for one another and our relationship never suffered. Good grief, it just occurred to me as I was writing this paragraph that my daddy was truly a genius! What better way to prepare a child to support his or her beliefs, than to make them think deeply, and in my case study the Scriptures intently for a good homespun argument! I'm speechless (that's a first).

During my teen years we fought like cats and dogs, but part of that was because we were so much alike – both of us as stubborn as mules! In all the shouting matches, in all the disagreements, I always respected him, even when I didn't show it. Because of the relationship we always had, I knew I could be completely honest with Daddy, even though he may disagree with me. He accepted me for who I am, and he loved me unconditionally – which was the only way my daddy knew how to love. My relationship with God would not be what it is today had I not had a dad that lived a life that showed me that I could trust my Heavenly Father.

One of my most terrifying experiences with Daddy occurred when I was nine years old. My grandmother had recently died, and my cousin Bobby and his family were visiting. Daddy was a smoker at that time, and on this particular day he began to choke on the cigarette smoke. We're not sure what caused it, but all he could do was inhale – not exhale. Bobby was somehow able to stop Daddy from choking. I wish I could tell you what he did, but I was too busy running around the backyard screaming to the top of my lungs "God save my Daddy!" That was also the day I realized I wasn't cut out to be the nurse I'd always dreamed of being, considering that most patients would frown on their nurse running down the hall screaming "God save the patient". Daddy quit smoking that day – cold turkey, no five-, ten-, or twelve-step plan. He just quit! This was in the 60's before it was popular to quit, and I think it was also before the Surgeon General told us how detrimental smoking was to our health.

Although I broke my daddy's heart when I chose not to go to college, he never told me – I heard it from another family member. What he did do was give me some really good advice: "If you're not going to college, go to work for Uncle Sam in a civilian capacity like your old man". Daddy served our country not only during WWII and the Korean War in the military, but also as a civilian once he was discharged. I took his advice, and no one was prouder of my accomplishments than my daddy as I climbed the ladder during my career. He retired as a Grade 11, Step 10 with almost 40 years service. I retired as a Grade 12, Step 10 with over 34 years service. I will never forget the look on his face, nor his comment when I got my Grade 12: "Well, your old man ended his career with two aces, and you'll end yours with an *acee-ducee*". Yep, that was the Deacon!!

Even as an adult, I loved spending time with Daddy and hearing stories of his childhood, the Great War, fish tales of his fishing trips with his brothers, and all the other stories he loved telling...over and over again. He lived a very rich and rewarding life, and he used humor to get him through most of it. If I had to state the one thing besides his faith in God that my Daddy taught me, it would be not to take myself too seriously. He didn't verbalize that to me, he lived it. Time after time, I saw him laugh, grin, or joke around during some of the most trying times of his life.

One such time was about a week after a family member died. Daddy had not yet gone back to work, but decided to go in for the going away party for a young trainee returning home to Pennsylvania. She'd been in Charleston for about six months working in the Comptroller's Office along side Daddy. The office had taken up a collection to purchase her a nice gift, but Daddy walked up to her with a smaller gift in his hand (and a twinkle in his eye). She broke out laughing as she unwrapped her box of grits. Later, she told Daddy she was surprised that he was able to joke around so soon after losing a loved one. I'll always remember Daddy's reply: "I laugh so I don't cry". Without saying it in words, Daddy lived my mantra: how we respond to our circumstances is our choice. He not only lived my mantra, he taught **me** how to live my mantra.

My Father's Day gift to Daddy in 2005 was to fly with him to Oklahoma City to visit his older brother. Dad hadn't flown since 9/11, and since I flew frequently, he wanted me to accompany him. Our flight was delayed. I was reading a book and Daddy was people watching...and, apparently, trashcan watching.

All the times I'd been in Hartsfield-Jackson waiting on flights, never one time had I heard the trashcans! But Daddy not only heard them, he investigated them! All of a sudden, I became aware that he wasn't sitting beside me any longer. I panicked, looked around, and found him walking around the trashcan nearest us, studying it from all angles. "Uh Daddy, what are you doing?" "I'm trying to figure out what the noise is." "What noise?" "This trash can makes a grinding noise ever so often, but I can't figure out what triggers it." About that time the trashcan made its noise, and I realized there must be a garbage compactor inside and told Daddy. "Well I KNOW THAT! But what triggers it? It doesn't happen every time someone throws something away." (I told you he'd been watching the trashcan.) "Maybe it's on a timer." "I bet you're right, I'm going to time it." And that's how we all now know that the garbage at Hartsfield-Jackson Airport in Atlanta, GA, is compacted every five minutes.

We finally boarded our plane and headed for Oklahoma. The weather (which had held us up to begin with) continued to be an issue all the way there, and I must admit there were times I was wishing that perhaps we'd waited just a little longer before leaving. Anyhow, we finally touched down for what was arguably the roughest landing I've ever experienced. As we were leaving the plane, Daddy realized the pilot was female. I knew what he was going to say even before we got to where she was standing. I knew it, and I couldn't stop it. "Oh, a female driver – no wonder it was such a rough trip." Did I say life with Daddy was interesting? Did I mention wanting to melt into the floor of the plane? When I shrieked "Daddy!" he smiled at her with that charming little twinkle in his eye, and said, "I'm only kidding, little lady, you did a fine job." Thank goodness, I didn't have to bail him out of jail for sexual harassment!!

An amazing story involving Daddy was decades in the

making. Many years ago in Macon, GA, he taught a young boy in Sunday school by the name of Hubert. Hubert grew up and became a Minister of Music in Macon. He had a young boy in his youth choir by the name of Eddie, who grew up and became a Minister of Music in Powder Springs, GA. Eddie had a young girl in his youth choir by the name of Jeri, who is my daughter, named for Daddy. That story just gives me chills!!

My absolute favorite trip with Daddy was in October 2009, when my husband Matthew and I took him to Washington to see the WWII Memorial. The Memorial itself is awesome enough, but it is even more moving to go there with someone who defended our country during those years. It is divided into areas depicting the Pacific Theater and European Theater, with smaller monuments of the various battles of each. The Government provided wheelchairs for those that needed them, and Daddy, along with several other brave and wonderful men, rolled along remembering their experiences. Occasionally they would engage in conversation with one another. We bought Daddy a baseball cap that read: WWII Veteran, which quickly became one of his prized possessions. He wore it everywhere, and someone would always come up to him, shake his hand, and thank him for his service. "I was just doing my job", was his humble reply.

In January of 2010 we heard the words no family wants to hear, "Mr. Barrington most likely has Alzheimer's". I can't even describe how heart broken I was. Oh, there had been red flags here and there, but none of us wanted to face the truth. For the next three years we watched Daddy ebb away. The son, the brother, the uncle, the soldier, the husband, the daddy, the granddaddy, the great-granddaddy, and the deacon – the finest man I've ever known. On January 1, 2013, he lost his battle to that awful disease.

I am so proud to have been "the deacon's daughter"! I would not be the person I am today without his influence in my life. Through all the ups and downs of my life, on all the roads that I traveled, my faith has sustained me. And that faith began with a little girl, watching her daddy live his faith – day in and day out. I am forever grateful to him. Thank you, Daddy, this "deacon's daughter" loves you.

MAXENE D. RAICES

　　Memoir and fiction writer Maxene Raices graduated with a Bachelor of Arts in Education (minoring in English), and her Masters of Education in Adult Communication, and earned her New York Secondary School Teacher's Certificate.

　　Her career includes ninth grade English teacher, human resource manager, and consultant with Fortune 500 organizations, where she led training programs to improve sales, leadership, and workforce effectiveness.

　　Maxene is the mother of two grown children, Linda and Trevor. Married to Lee McGuire, her blended family also includes two step children and a total of seven grandchildren.

　　She is currently writing her memoir, and has published an excerpt in the *Atlanta Journal Constitution Personal Journeys* as their first short story contest winner in 2015.

Shawl of Ivy

    She walks up and down the street, muttering, barefoot, greasy hair dangling in wisps down her neck. Her clothes hang from her starved meth ridden body as if the hangar was never removed. Her teeth are rotted and yellow from the drugs, tobacco and coffee. Her intelligence is fogged like a mirror in a sauna: clouded by years of self-abuse. Her world is full of demons and shadows and a nagging need to survive it all. Turning tricks provides enough cash to keep the cycle going.
    Her mother steps out of the shack that they have called home for all of her daughter's thirty years of life. Ivy curls around the fence posts and reaches out to the old pine trees that serve as a cooling umbrella over the shack they call home.
    Pam's mother's hair is arranged in a neat bun and her pressed uniform gives the impression that she cares about order and cleanliness. What has kept her going? How has she managed to plod to work in her battered Ford each day, knowing her daughter is left behind to wander the streets muttering, picking people's garbage, stealing from flea markets and selling herself behind churches and school yards? The burger place where she works has been her escape from her daughter and her home: a place to feel valued, where life is predictable and orderly.
    Pam was once a star university student, studying engineering. Her childhood memories were of her hard working single mother who raised her and her brother, struggling to bring food to the table and stay optimistic about life. Early on, Pam realized that life was a struggle. She had only fleeting memories of her father who stormed around in a

drunken stupor, yelling and abusing her mother. Her brother left home at eighteen and joined the Army. Pam lost herself in her books. In high school, she found herself getting attention from a rough group of kids who thought she was a nerd. She took it hard and looked for a way out. Her studies helped, but a nagging emptiness kept her on edge, feeling like a trapped animal, unloved, invisible, trying to survive the emptiness.

Then life took a dramatic turn. She was invited to a party at a frat house and found herself indulging in euphoria as she tried to be part of the group. She took a few tokes of a pipe. A dark, powerfully built young man named Charles stroked her hair as she experienced a floating sensation. This sensation of light headedness was new to her; somewhere deep inside she equated it with love. He asked if she'd like to try something that would make her feel even better.
In her haze, she said "Sure, why not?" throwing her head back, exposing her slender neck and small breasts behind her black school t-shirt. She followed his instructions, and snorted the line on the glass table top. The room became a whirlwind of movement. She found herself laughing as she'd never laughed before as she took the ride of her life without going anywhere.

She crawled out of the frat house the next morning, leaving a rumpled bed that still contained the young man from the night before. She wasn't sure where she was or what had happened to her. She tried to remember details, but they didn't come. She just knew she needed to get out into the fresh air.

In the days and weeks that followed, she was drawn back to the frat house to recapture the sense of euphoria and wrap herself in the chemically induced feeling of love and warmth of Charles. Soon, they were discussing running away from the strain of school and finding a way to live on their own.

Focusing was very difficult. Over the next few weeks, she knew that things had dramatically changed. She couldn't quite define it, but her gut told her she had crossed over into another world. Then she realized she was pregnant.

They dropped out of school, and established a home base in the basement of an elderly woman's home, who charged them a nominal fee if they would do chores for her. A baby girl came screaming into the world and life seemed almost normal. They scraped by with odd jobs. Pam took the baby with her each day as she cleaned houses. Charles got a job working at a recycling plant, sorting used jars, newspapers, cans and cardboard boxes.

A year went by, and Pam was pregnant again, weighed

down with the realization that life had always been hard and unrelenting. Charles was getting irritated with everything. "Can't you get the kid to stop crying??" he screamed. "I need to some space and time to think this whole arrangement through. I gotta get out of here."

He complained about their cramped quarters. He started to disappear during the night, leaving Pam to fend for herself with two small children. The only time they didn't fight was when Charles took out his baggy of drugs and they sniffed their way into oblivion after the children were in bed.

The old lady upstairs was becoming aware that there was fighting going on; she could hear loud voices, and stomping and got worried and afraid. Soon Child Protective Services showed up to inspect the basement apartment and assess the safety of the home for the children.

They discovered meth in cupboards. Charles showed up in a haze of drugs and alcohol. Pam looked disheveled. The apartment was strewn with pizza boxes, stale cigarette butts piled high in makeshift ashtrays. Two babies were crawling around in filthy diapers. The children were taken away to be placed in foster care, and Charles was arrested on charges of drug use.

The old lady asked Pam to leave.

"But I have no place to go."

"Sorry, but I can't have you here anymore after what just happened. I'm embarrassed that I let it go on for as long as I did. Those poor babies..."

She packed her meagre belongings that evening and wandered the city streets, looking for a cheap place to sleep. A hotel with a half lit blue neon sign welcomed her in. Sleep on a lumpy bed with threadbare sheets was a welcomed escape from her day. She tried to keep up with cleaning houses over the next few weeks, but soon found she had no energy to continue. Besides, she couldn't afford to keep her car, and it was soon repossessed. She became desperate.

She found herself in alleys offering herself up to strange men for cash. Occasionally, someone would hand her drugs instead. She had hit rock bottom. She needed to go home.

Her mother had lost touch with her when she dropped out of school two years earlier. She too had been cleaning houses and found it was wearing her down. She managed to land a job at the local hamburger joint; a real job meant less back breaking days and included a clean uniform and a steady paycheck. Her burgundy Ford was still working and could take her to work, but now it groaned and creaked from old age.

The knock on the rickety door took Pam's mother by surprise.

"Who's there?" she shouted from her tiny kitchen where she was making a cup of tea.

"Ma, it's me: Pam! Can I come in?"

"Pam? Yes! Yes! Of course!"

Her mother opened the front door and stood in shock as she saw a wraith that sounded like her daughter. Pam had lost at least twenty five pounds and was all angles. Her grimy clothes looked like she had slept in them for weeks. Her running shoes were torn. What was most shocking was the transformation of her smile. What was once a shy tentative smile had now turned into a crooked grimace of rotted teeth.

"Oh my God. What has happened to you? Why didn't you let me know where you were?"

"I guess I wanted to be out of the house and on my own. I thought I was in love and loved and that everything would work out."

She lowered her head and stared at the floor, unable to face her mother.

Pam entered the home that she'd left two years ago, and her mother went to work, filling the bathtub and finding some clean clothes for her daughter. The swirl of warm water enveloping her emaciated body was as close to a spiritual experience as Pam had had since the first time she did drugs.

Months passed. Her mother left for her job each morning and Pam tried to figure out what to do with her empty life. She grieved the loss of her children. She sometimes bellowed out loud at the loss of her purpose. Eventually, the pull to that familiar meth high was too strong for her to resist. She soon found dealers who would sell her small quantities of marijuana to keep her going. When that was gone and she needed cash, she would wander off and get caught in the back of some stranger's car, doing "favors" and occasionally getting arrested and ending up in the local jail. Police officers joked about her seeing her repeat appearances at their facility every few months.

"She's back."

They'd pick her up from the streets after seeing her soliciting. After withdrawing from her most recent drug high, the light in her eyes would start to gleam. A good meal, a shower or two and a change into clean prison garb made her almost presentable. She slept like there's no tomorrow. And then they would have to release her.

"Here ya go Pam. We can only hold ya for so long. It's the law. Try and clean up yer act, will ya?"

The sergeant was getting tired of providing his jail as a B & B to her.

She had returned to the dark place that her life had become and the cycle repeated itself, swirling in the unthinkable cesspool that was now her daily routine. With her mother as anchor, she could survive just barely inside the shack, peeking out the door each day to discover a world she no longer understood. Her will had been broken; her mind was fogged by the drugs.

Only this time, it was different. She was picked up five days earlier and had once again started to be back into her old routine. She had showered and was ready for prison breakfast. The sergeant approached the cell with a dower look on his face, eyes lowered. She'd had almost a week to recover from her last meth high and was feeling pretty good about getting out and rejoining her mother.

"Pam, I have to tell ya something," the sergeant growled, speaking slowly in almost a whisper while shuffling his feet as he looked into her eyes. "Something bad has happened. Yer mom had a heart attack and passed last night." His eyes fixed on the fragile woman in the cell.

"What? What did you just say? No... no... no!"

Pam moaned and began to rock on her cell bed, holding herself and shaking her head in disbelief. She rocked back and forth, jumping up from the bed and pacing, shaking her head and muttering,

"No.... no.... that's not true! You're lying to me!"

Pam's ramshackle house with the old air conditioner stuck out of the window is now silent. Pam's collection of old lawn furniture, a chain link ladder from an old boat, and various knickknacks that she had scoffed from local flea markets and garage sales, that littered the porch are all gone. The street is slowly transforming with old country cottages being torn down to make way for new homes. Pam's brother, who has been living on the other side of the country, has received the news of their mother's death and struggles to decide what to do with the property and what to do about his sister. She has been released from the jail and transferred to a mental institution where she receives counseling and wanders the hallways, interacting with no one, watching as other patients rock and moan or stare into space. Will her brother break the cycle and decide to bring her into his home? Not likely. But if he can't afford to support her rehabilitation, he knows she may end up on the streets for good.

Pam's mom's car still sits in the dirt driveway, waiting for another day to be driven to the burger place. But no one exits the house, bun neatly tied, uniform pressed. The ivy that has surrounded the property for years wrapping around trees, twisting up fence posts and across the ground has slowly begun to expand its ownership across the freewheeling garden, reaching out to caress the tires of the burgundy Ford. Slowly, the green tendrils lace themselves through the hubcaps, onto the tires, reaching tirelessly to engulf the vehicle and hold it prisoner. To make it disappear.

Three months have passed and Pam is still housed in an institution where white coated men and women try to reach her, to get her beyond declarations of "No! She can't be dead! Why isn't she visiting me?"

Every day is predictable and without exception. The burgundy car is a permanent fixture in the front of the shack, collecting Spring's yellow pollen dust, growing moldy inside as the rains begin and as Summer approaches, enveloped in a green shawl of ivy. The street is quiet now and the ramshackle house sighs as the final cycle of life envelops it. The only thing left of its inhabitants rests in the memory of neighbors passing by as they walk their dogs or head to work, wondering what ever happened to Pam, recounting the struggles of her mother and watching as Nature consumes history.

CINDY DU GAN

    Cindy earned her BS in Education, and spent 33 years as a teacher, working with a variety of age groups.
    She has always loved reading and writing both fiction and poetry, but her first piece of writing was a children's story, based on a question her oldest son asked when he was a toddler.
    Cindy has taken three creative writing classes in the past year, and her pursuit is buoyed by her recently retired husband and three grown children, who encourage her to pursue her dream of writing.
"I also have two grandchildren who love to read and can be my toughest critics," she says.
    She loves writing and plans to continue in this pursuit. She says she is particularly enamored with the "What If...?"

What If I Knew?

What if I knew that today would be the last day I would open my eyes?

The last time I would ever look at a sky so blue it hurt to see it;

The last time I would feel the hot sun caressing and soaking my body

With warmth both soothing and energizing;

The last time I would hear the laughter of children while they play.

 Such haunting music!

Never to see and smell the flowers all around,

Could they have ever before been such a rich color?

To touch the soft supple skin of a new baby

Fragrant, warm and fresh from its bath.

Never to walk the richly scented woods pungent earth and green

Making an intoxicating wild perfume.

Feeling the cool from the trees, a respite from the warmth of the day.

What if I knew as I looked at the bright light of the stars

Beckoning in the forever blackness,

That tonight would be the last night I would close my eyes?

Would I try to fight that which I could not fight - not win?

Would I gracefully submit, embracing that which cannot be changed -

Not in a million lifetimes?

Accept the inevitable with sadness and loss for all not seen and felt.

What if I knew?

GRETCHEN K. CORBIJN

Gretchen K. Corbijn began taking writing classes at FoxTale Book Shoppe in January 2014, but her love of words and writing began in the third grade with a composition her teacher raved about. "I enjoyed the escape, she enjoyed the detail," Gretchen says.

After graduating from high school, Gretchen earned her Paralegal Certification through Boston University, and her Bachelors Degree in Criminal Justice from Brevard Community College. She is an Accounts Receivables professional by day, and a Romance and Young Adult fiction writer by night.

Gretchen lives in Woodstock, Georgia, with her husband, Eddie, son, Beckett, and two cats, Hermione and Adso.

She plans to publish her book, Regent's Park in 2016. The following are excerpts from her forthcoming novel...

A Comfort In The Night
A "Regent's Park" Short Story

    Willa inhaled sharply, feigning off her anxiety as she finished packing for a client meeting in New York. Her camera bag and portfolio lay on the bed along with her small suitcase, and she wondered if maybe she should delay getting back into the field. An excuse quickly filled her mind; Molly was still mending from Jack's psychotic break and the chaos that followed. Molly still had anxiety and would sometimes have attacks. Tom knew how to handle them, and he honestly handled them better than Willa did. It was just as good excuse as any, being the overprotective mother, and it was falling flat. The only thing holding her back now was herself if she allowed it.
    The laughter and screeching she heard coming from Molly's room eased Willa's uneasiness. Tom, in his socked feet, slid by the open master suite door and slammed into the wall, a giggling Molly followed suit slamming into him. He met Willa's eyes and smiled, before he hollered, and took off running down the hall again. Molly, breathless from the laughter and running, was once again right behind him.
    Willa laughed at herself, squashing her nerves. She had left Molly overnight on a few occasions with her parents since the attack. Molly was usually fine and had nary an incident, yet her thoughts still ran rampant. *It will only be three days, in a different country, across an ocean. Absolutely nothing to worry about.* Willa quickly quelled the sarcastic thought from her head; she trusted Tom with Molly.
    She peered out the doorway, catching a glimpse of the two, now dancing on the hardwood, and she felt her heart settle. "It

will be alright," she said to herself. "If anything, he'll wear *her* out and she'll sleep well for him."

Willa heard the knock on the front door, and Tom's announcement that his best friend Luke had arrived with the car. The nerves in her stomach flipped as she watched Luke enter and Tom come toward her down the hallway. "Are you alright?" he whispered, seeing the fear on her face.

Willa nodded, "I'm good, I'm good."

He slipped around her and grabbed her luggage, his eyes never leaving hers. "She'll be fine," he assured her for what may have been the millionth time. "And if you don't want to go, I understand. There's no one forcing you, Wills."

His assurance and the endearment she loved calmed her, yet her eyes diverted down to her wringing hands, "I want to do this. It will be good for me. I need to get back into the field. Once I'm on the plane, I'll relax, I'm sure of it."

He tucked a finger under her chin and brought her eyes back to his, "Your anxiety is valid. It's normal. You're just mad you're going to miss all the fun." She couldn't help but laugh, and he kissed her softly, "And I am going to miss kissing those lips."

"Three days," she reminded him with a smile and a touch to his cheek as Luke poked his head into the hallway.

"Break it up you two, no time for a snog fest, there's a plane to catch," Luke said with a sarcastic tone as they both stifled a giggle.

The light traffic en route to Heathrow gave Willa more time to quiz Tom on what to do if anything were to happen to Molly. He let her ramble, knowing it had to be done to clear her mind. He gently reminded her that he had lists of phone numbers and that she had an open ended ticket that would get her home early if she deemed necessary.

"If she has a nightmare, just ride it out with her. She hasn't had one in a while, so maybe we're past that?" Willa sighed as she stroked Molly's hair, trying to remember anything that he could possibly forget or fret about.

Tom looked down at Molly, who was nestled against him watching a movie on the iPad, and looked back at Willa, "Love, I know her fairly well. I've been present for several nightmares and know what to do if one happens. She'll be okay."

Willa exhaled loudly as he took her hand to calm her nerves. "I love you," she reminded. "I'm sorry I'm pestering you."

He kissed her cheek, "Love, you are not pestering. You're being a mum."

Willa smiled at him and pulled Molly close to her, "Thank you."

He leaned over the little girl and stole a kiss from Willa, "I love you," he affirmed. "Now focus on your meeting, which you know, you'll knock them dead."

~*~*~*~*~*~*

"Molly, you make sure he behaves. I want a full story when I get back," Willa said on bended knee, straightening her daughter's jumper, doing her best to keep her emotion in check.

Molly smiled at her mother, "Okay momma. I'll take good care of Tom."

Willa blinked back the tears as she stood and Tom took the three of them in an embrace, kissing her. "Go," he assured her. "We'll both be here to greet you in three days."

She forced the smile, kissed them both as Tom helped heft her bag up on her shoulder and said her goodbyes. They waited until she was through the security line, then turned and waved once more.

The two glanced at each other, and he kneeled to match her height, "What do you say we go have some fun?"

The little girls eye widened, "What are we gonna do?" she asked excitedly.

"Whatever you wish to do."

She thought for a minute, "Can we get ice cream?"

He chuckled, "First stop, ice cream."

His intention was to spoil her, and he wanted to make sure this first solo time together was special. He had memorable things lined up to enjoy this bonding "Molly and Tom" time. She took his hand and gleefully skipped to keep up with his stride as the two set off.

The afternoon consisted of the promised ice cream and then a stroll around the London Zoo. Tom took in her laughter and her amazement as she watched the animals. He loved how she took his hand and excitedly pointed things out to him. He hung on every word she said as she explained lions and tigers, he laughed when she roared, and calmed her when one of the big cats roared loudly in her proximity. The pair spent hours walking, observing and laughing.

Tom's own nervousness began to wane. He wouldn't fathom the thought of telling Willa that he had a bit of apprehension. Fatherhood was a new role for him, and he thrived in the excitement it contained. Molly came into his life, stole his heart, and wrapped herself around his finger. A child not his by birth yet his by love. After the chaos of her earlier childhood, he vowed to give the stability they deserved. Molly adored him, and their bond was tight. She tugged on his sleeve, breaking his thoughts, ready to explore new things and he felt six years old right along with her.

Tom gave in to her in the gift shop as her eyes locked on a stuffed tiger. They had take-away of fish and chips in Regent's, and he listened attentively to her wide-eyed stories about her tutor, dance class, her new love for horses, and the tales her bright imagination conjured as the afternoon wore on. A visit to the playground as the sun began to set and a stroll through the gardens on the way home ended their perfect park day together.

Molly had her bath, and Tom read and reenacted stories until Willa called to check in, letting them know that she had arrived safely in New York. She chided him about bedtime, and he scoffed, knowing that she could do nothing about it from across the pond. It was after all "Molly and Tom" time. It was times like this that he hoped, when Willa's photography career picked back up and when he had a break from his own, would bond them, creating special memories. Memories he knew her father Jack would have never made, memories that Tom was determined to make.

They finished their story, and he tucked her in, kissing her head. "Tom," she whispered, slipping under her covers as he turned off her light and switched on the nightlight.

"Yea, Sweet Pea?"

"I had a great time today, I can't wait for tomorrow."

"So did I, love. Tomorrow will be even better!"

She smiled as she cuddled up with her doll and new tiger, and he leaned down and kissed her forehead. "Good night, Tom."

"Good night, Sweet Pea."

Tom went about his usual activities. He checked his emails, talked with Luke to make sure his tickets to the theatre would be ready, and that his tea reservations with Molly were set. He got in a quick workout, showered, and decided to settle himself down for the night. Sleep came quickly for him, keeping up with a six year old no matter how great of shape you were in was exhausting.

Molly's screams were deafening, terrifying, and heartbreaking all at once. Tom, in all his years as a runner, never expected to move so fast and thought he may have actually flown to Molly's room. As he switched the light on he saw her sitting up, still trembling and panting, her hair soaked from sweat. Her eyes still unable to focus, searching frantically for something, anything to focus on.

"I'm right here, Sweet Pea," he whispered as he sat on the edge of the bed, Molly clutching him the millisecond he was within reach.

She was soaked and shaking. The nightmares that were consistent after the attack had waned considerably, and in fact this was the first one in months. They had thought they may have been a thing of the past, as therapies really worked in helping Molly get past Jack's abandonment and attack on her and her mother.

Tonight was very different.

He calmed her, clutching her to his chest, trying to soothe her trembling. "I'm right here," he reminded as she let out a choking sob, her hold on him becoming even tighter.

Tom stroked her hair, feeling her calm a bit, although he could still feel her heart racing against him. Molly took a few deep breaths, still clinging to him, and Tom held her closer, hoping the embrace would give her the comfort she so desperately needed.

"He left me all alone in the park again," Molly's weak voice squeaked out.

His heart, which was already breaking because she had to again be disturbed by memories, dropped and shattered. "You're alright," he reassured, his own memory now recalling pulling her wet, scared, and cold from the playground that horrible rainy night, "I have you."

Tom let her sob, hating that when she had the terrors they were so vivid, and there was nothing he could do but hold her and let her work it out. She calmed slowly, pulling away from the embrace and searched out his eyes seeking comfort. He tucked her hair behind her ear as she whispered, "I'm okay."

Tom exhaled, then kissed her hair realizing that her sheets were soaked along with her nightclothes. "Come on, let's get you comfortable again."

He helped her pick out a new nightgown and he stripped her sheets as she went to change. He was about to put new sheets on her bed when the continued look of distress on her face as she reentered the room gripped his heartstrings. He thought quickly of a calming method his own mum would use on him when he was upset as a child, "How about a glass of milk and a biscuit?"

She forced a smile, nodded, and followed him out to the kitchen. She sat in a chair, hands folded in her lap, legs swinging, and he watched her as she still processed that dream; swiping at stray tears as she waited for the snack. It had to have been the trip to the playground that triggered it. Her subconscious still connecting similar areas with terror. Tom put a small glass of milk in front of her and himself, and a small plate of cookies, and sat opposite her. "Do you want to talk to your mum?"

She shook her head, and muttered, "No," then sipped her milk, her little fingers fidgeting with the biscuit. "Tom? Are you going to leave us someday too?"

He forced a smile and swallowed hard, keeping the emotion that swelled down. "Oh Sweet Pea, I plan to be around for many, many years, and watch you grow into a beautiful young woman."

"I don't want you to go."

"I'll be here for you, always."

"Forever?"

"For as long as you'll let me."

Molly sighed, and nibbled on her treat and he assumed she was satisfied with the answer he gave her. She rose from her chair and crawled into his lap, once again embracing him, snuggling tight to his chest. "I promise you I will take good care of you. I fully intend to keep that promise to you. I will always be here for you, Molly."

She wrapped her arms around his neck, and yawned. Molly was getting comfortable to sleep again. She settled against his chest and in her small voice asked, "Tom, can I stay with you tonight?"

His answer was immediate, "Of course."

The biscuits and the half drank glasses of milk could wait until morning. The sheets that needed to be laundered and changed, had the same fate. He tucked his arm underneath her and carried her, only stopping to pick up her pillow, doll, and tiger to the bedroom he shared with her mother. He tucked her into Willa's side of the bed, Molly opting to sleep on her mother's pillow, the scent of Willa giving her daughter added comfort. Tom switched on the nightlight, kissed her hair, and crawled into bed himself.

Molly was half asleep, eyes drowsy, cuddled in blankets and stuffed friends when she reached out and took Tom's hand. "I love you, Daddy," she yawned.

Molly's words rang in his ears like a symphony. "I love you too, Molly."

He watched as she drifted off to sleep, and he finally let his own tears escape him.

She was *his* little girl.

Regent's Park - Conversations of the Heart
A Tom and Willa One-Shot

"What you've got there?" Tom asked fresh from the shower with a chuckle under his breath when he saw that Willa had scrambled into the t-shirt he had worn the night prior.

She shook the small box she was holding and the chalky hard contents bounced inside, "Candy," She sassed, crossing her legs and studying a tiny heart before popping it into her mouth. The crunch she made through her teeth made him wince a bit, "They're an American treat for Valentine's Day. Little bitty hearts. They have charming sayings on them."

"Is that so?" he said with peaked interest, "What kind of sayings?"

Willa shrugged coyly, "Sweet little things, cute little things. Cheeky. Little. Things," she started aligning a trio of hearts on her leg from her ankle to her thigh, word side up, as he sat himself down on the bed next to her.

Tom picked up a pink little heart that was square on her ankle and held it between his fingers, "Oh La La," he laughed softly, "I'm sure that's alluding to our Parisian adventure."

"Perhaps, that's our official re-start technically. There's very good memories there." she said with a grin as she watched him place the tiny heart in his mouth

He waggled his eyebrows as he also reminisced, "Yes, incredibly lovely memories," he hummed as his fingers walked from her ankle to her knee where the next heart waited. He turned the yellow heart with the bold neon pink writing towards him and he smiled. A smile that reached his eyes as he searched for hers, "Love Me Tender," he read, "One thing my gorgeous girl never has to worry about."

Willa returned the smile, feeling her heart flutter at his words and a blush rising in her cheeks. These little moments, as sickly sweet as the candy they shared never grew tiresome. Flirting was something almost entirely new to her, and Tom was an excellent teacher. "You say that so confidently." she said, with a roll to her eyes.

"If there's anything I am more confident about, even more than stage or screen, is loving you," was his reply, his nose in the air and said with complete British stuffiness.

She giggled, "Charmer, "mocking playfully as his fingers continued their climb up her leg. He winked as his hand crept under the hem of the t-shirt, brushing the skin near the edge of her panties, eliciting a gasp from her, "and cheeky."

He cocked an eyebrow, and his fingers deftly removed the remaining heart that sat on her thigh. The little blue heart made him purse his lips together, nearly silencing him. He leaned in and kissed her sweetly, the taste of the candy on his lips, "What? A piece of candy shut you up?" she laughed softly into his lips.

"Little heart, big meaning." he replied

Her hand cupped his face, his eyes soulful and endearing and she could have sworn they may had glistened with tears, "Well it's true, you are."

He looked down at the piece of candy in the palm of his hand, "Soul Mate" it read and he whispered it softly to her. He placed Willa's hands in his, clasping them together along with that little blue heart, and brought them to his chest. She felt the rhythm of his own heart beating under her hand. *"Hear my soul speak: The very instant that I saw you, did my heart fly to your service."* he whispered in her ear. The quote from Shakespeare, fitting with everything that they had been through made her breath hitch as she felt the emotion well in her throat. "Who's speechless now?" He added.

She laughed and granted him another roll of her eyes as she stole another kiss from his lips, "Charming wanker." she smiled.

He kissed her forehead, their hands still at his heart, "For life." he sighed, "My soul mate."

Oh The Pain
A "Regent's Park" One Shot

"Are you going to get out of bed today, love?" Tom asked as he finished dressing for whatever meeting that he may have had that day.

Willa groaned and burrowed herself in the mass of blankets on the bed, "No, go away."

"Go away?" He replied a tone of uncertainty and sarcasm mixed in his voice, "what did I do?"

"Nothing," was her muffled response, "It's not what you did, it's what you *have*."

She felt the mattress dip with his weight as he sat himself next to the mound of blanket mixed human, "What I *have*?"

Willa pulled the heap down to show her face, hair disheveled, eyes slanted in her meanest expression, "A penis."

He chuckled and he raised his eyebrows, "Not that you've ever complained about that before, though I won't be a total wanker... I'm assuming it's "that time?"

She groaned again covering her face, "Go away, Tom," she bellowed from beneath the blankets.

"Oh but I'm envious. Your cycle means the creation of life. So feminine and beautiful..." he was rambling and he soon became aware of a blue eyed death stare. "And you're in pain and uncomfortable and it looks like you want to throttle me."

"It's crossing my mind, Thomas."

"Hmmm, I have an idea."

The weight on the mattress shifted again as he got up and Willa felt his hand on her shoulder. Tom would have sworn she hissed at him like an angry feral cat. He stepped down the stairs, having had two sisters he knew well enough where his boundary lie with Willa and he wasn't going to push it with silliness or sarcasm. He rummaged in the kitchen, then the medicine cabinet creating a little tray with care items. He waited for the kettle of tea to finish and with a smile and a feeling of pride within himself he bravely went back to the bedroom.

Willa was still in her blanket fort, and he could tell she was in pain by the way she was curled underneath them.

"Wills, love." he whispered hoping the endearment he used for her would ease her some.

"I thought you were leaving," she growled, "Please just leave me alone for a few hours."

"I will, but I've brought you some things," he explained as he set the tray on the night table.

She crawled out from her comfort zone and looked at the tray. Hot tea, Hob Nobs, a couple of pieces of Mozart chocolate, a heating pad, paracetamol and a vase with daisies all presented before her, "I wanted to make sure you were taken care of and comfortable before I left. I hope it's enough, or if there's something else you need I'll go get it."

She pulled herself into a seated position, her hair even more disheveled than before, and looked at him with apologetic eyes. "You did this for me? Your nasty, evil, menstruating girlfriend?"

"My beautiful, kind hearted, pained, and uncomfortable girlfriend." he replied as she felt the tears well, and he took off to the bathroom and returned quickly with a box of tissues, "Almost forgot."

She chuckled, and dabbed her eyes, "I'm sorry for being a complete bitch."

"Oh hush. You're not feeling well, and while I could never empathise with you, I could at least sympathise and treat you with the love and respect you deserve."

She smiled and put her hand to his face, "You take such great care of me."

He stole a kiss from her lips, "You're my Wills, there's nothing that I wouldn't do for you."

She sighed, knowing how true that statement was, "I'm very lucky."

"Luck aside, let's get you comfortable," he said as he checked an incoming text message, "I'll pick up Molly from school, and I'll be close to home if you should need anything. My first meeting was cancelled so if there's anything you need..."

She looked at him guilt heavy in her eyes. His selflessness making her regret her grumpiness towards him "Could you just lay with me?"

His smiled reached his eyes, and he held the comforter up so she could get comfortable underneath them. She curled up to him and his large warm hand splayed out on her bloated belly and subconsciously began to rub circles. The warmth of his skin against hers, and the movement of his hand were helping to alleviate the pain she was feeling.

"You have no idea how much that is helping." Willa said letting the comfort of his touch wash over her.

She shifted closer to him, a sign that her pain was lessening. Her breathing deepened and he knew that she was finally relaxing, "It should be a man's nature to care for their partner during this time. It used to be, perhaps. Childbirth, motherhood, pain and discomfort all thrown onto you. The least we could do is show the stronger sex a little compassion."

She laughed at his sincerity, sleep heavy on her voice "Just for that I *won't* throttle you today, wanker."

TERRI SLONE

Terri Slone grew up in Southern California and was transplanted to Alabama for a few years before landing happily in Atlanta.

Now living in Canton, Georgia, with her significant other and his son, she spends her time on photography and writing, after a career in sales and private label manufacturing for the gift industry.   Her products have been featured on the Today show and in Glamour magazine. She has spent time fundraising for start-up non-profits and has a passion for animal welfare.

Her canine, Donald Lee, is a three-legged boy found on the I-285 on-ramp at Donald Lee Holowell Parkway in southwest Atlanta.

Emma

Emma had round doe like eyes and a pointed nose poking through her abundant brown and blonde mane. Her upright ears poked through all that hair informing her acute hearing. She studied everyone up at the loud clapboard house through all the fear laid down like tire marks over her. She might have been satisfied with death. All she knew was dark wet dirt and lots of cold hiding under the building on the back of the property. She was identified as "Nose" because that's all the residents up front ever saw of her.

After a period of time she could not have known, she had been taken by the authorities and locked up. There was no difference in the fear she felt from the neglect and abuse and the new place except for the relentless noise and the confinement. She compressed herself in the back of the locked space, shaking.

The shelter authorities called and asked me to take her in. She needed all that had happened replaced with new to begin to learn trust in people. Good food, regular hours, constant kindness were required, and a new identity. She still shook in waves, days later, but had learned quickly to like the food and be fine with the others that had come to be there in their various levels of distress. She looked like a little lion and walked silently like one. Her eyes were watchful, sad, and there was a draw to her. She, a scarred creature lit a palpable desire to repair what had been done.

We had planned that trip to Miami a few weeks before the call to take her. Emma had been with me about two weeks when we set out. She had grown comfortable sleeping curled up next to me in the fancy bed with the ironed sheets. Her small brown body had stopped shaking when she crawled close. It was very comforting to me to have her still, less fearful self next to me. I was certain she had never slept next to a human. I had been sleeping alone for a while in our house in the big bed. She felt like a gift to me. I was reasonably sure about her adjustment to the house. I had Norma to handle everything at home when I was away. I trusted her completely.

    I loved Miami and took great pleasure finding trendy dinner spots, the best shopping, and great tickets to the tennis tournament. I liked the Latin vibe, the water and certain sun. It reminded me of growing up in Southern California, but with better architecture. My husband was too old for nightlife, and I had no interest in it. I was becoming old, too. I had become conservative in every way, ensconced in the moneyed life. I lived like I was taken care of, privileged, but in reality, I was half of all the making of enough to satisfy us for life. What he did after we sold the business that built it all, was on him.

    We took our jet on all our trips. If there was one defining feature of having been successful, it was that. Despite the extraordinary expense of it, he had persuaded me of it's value. He had created a business to justify it. There was an understanding that he was smarter than everyone else, and he rolled out deals like he was teflon and nothing could go wrong. So we set out for Miami in the jet.

    Emma found her way out of the secure iron fence custom built around the house and pool shortly after we arrived in Miami. I had set the width of the bars to contain all the dogs by measuring their shoulders. Her fur disguised how small she really was. Sacha, his part time daughter, called about six pm, after we had arrived at the Ritz and were enjoying an evening cocktail at the club level at the Ritz Key Biscayne. Norma had called both his adult children, and they had all three scouted the neighborhood for Emma. I was the one who had embraced saving them. I was a little surprised and enormously grateful they participated in helping try to find her. Saving dogs was really all on me. Our agreement was I wouldn't have children, but I could have as many dogs as I wanted. When we left for Miami, there were six, with Emma as a foster, made seven.

    When Sacha called, I knew what had to be. Within a couple of hours, I was home walking the street with a flashlight. I believed I would be back in Miami in the morning. She would hear me calling for her with food and she would step out of the woods. I was sure.

The next morning a women out walking claimed a sighting based on a picture, then became uncertain, saying she may have seen a red fox. Three of us walked all morning with another driving looking for a sighting. The lots, all beautifully wooded were one to two acres each, and left mostly alone to preserve the trees despite fallen ones and the resulting power outage after every rain. I found a neighbor who claimed to have seen her on their property, and allowed us to continue to look. Animal control provided us with a trap used catch strays in the field. We set it out at once.

My husband found a stray of his own back at the hotel in Miami. She would show up later on the only credit card bill of his I ever opened, and change the course of my life.

We had dated first, then became a business partnership. He liked money. In fact that was his most successful relationship. He had a sense about making it I'd never seen before. We started from nothing. I was the backyard gate hanging off the hinge, with no grass on either side of it. Untapped talent that had been running for years from loss. He had his own losses, ex-wives, money, prison time. He told me about all of it, right away. I believed in the hard work the 360 days of the 365 we were together the first year. I had never had a man pursue me so doggedly. I did not know until later what alcoholism was.

After the first week I set a time lapse camera in front of the trap. I called The Pet Detective, to track her, with his own dogs, twice. After nothing turned up, I called a pet psychic. I had never been to, or talked to a psychic. I couldn't sleep, couldn't give up. The woman, whose name I have deliberately forgotten actually sounded quite normal. She told what Emma could see, and I pretended it was at the private school near us, and that she was looking at a groundskeeper, or a security guard. So I called The Pet Detective again. A couple of days later she told me Emma was too scared and weak to look for food, and was close to dying. She told me to send her my love to help her cross over, so I did.

My marriage lasted another two years till the day I agreed to return to the big house after a six month separation. I maintained a personal policy from my upbringing never to open another person's mail. That day I made an exception. When I saw a week's charge for the penthouse suite at the Mandarin Oriental in Miami, and a plane ticket in her name, I crossed over.

The Steves

All the Steves marked firsts. After the first couple of Steves, I should have learned to take a detour when they showed up. I guess I couldn't help myself.

Third grade was my favorite year in school. I loved my teacher's soft eyes and comforting roundness. It helped a lot that I made straight A's. I stayed after school once to be with her, without telling my Mom, leading to a long walk home up a dangerous street toward our duplex in Inglewood, California. My Mom had taught me to keep my head down and look straight ahead, never speaking to anyone on the street. About halfway up the concrete hill, a older man pulled his car close, rolled down the window and asked if I needed a ride. I was certain to say no and keep going. It seemed like he followed me for about five minutes, trying to persuade me it was smarter to take a ride in that dangerous neighborhood. He was strange enough to make me certain of following my instructions about strangers. Now I wonder if he might have been the real first Steve.

My elementary school that third grade year had the usual southern California playground activities, hopscotch, jump rope, tetherball and dodgeball. In the middle of the playground was a wall painted like desert dirt with markings of a court around it. Less ball was played on it, but lots of ink had found a place there. Small hands had written small words about eyeball level. Steve G. was in the 4th grade and slightly taller than the rest of us. He had smooth thick brown hair parted and sloped across his perfect olive skin. He walked over to the dirty beige handball wall and pointed to a particular word. "Do you know what that says?" "No" now three of us girls replied. "It says fuck" he informed us, proud that he knew. "Do you know what it means?", he continued. I backed away, not wanting to appear stupid, but unable to stop myself from saying "no" quietly. Later, I felt pretty good about my curiosity at lunch break. When I got home from school, I decided to ask my buttoned down, had me too young Mom what it meant. She was quite forceful in her questioning about where I had heard the word and from whom. Fortunately she was satisfied with my answer so I received only a stern warning never to use the word. I never did get to know what it meant. A couple of days later, Steve G. gave me my first kiss right on the mouth. He didn't ask permission, or give any kind of warning, and I liked it, Didn't tell Mom anything about that day. The kiss and learning my first four letter word were about equal. Thanks Steve.

    About age fifteen, my Dad went through a camping phase. I don't know how my perfectly groomed Mom tolerated those Southern California desert weekends motorcycling. Our four person family would load up the travel trailer with enough food and junk to last the long two and a half days. The group would float from ten to twenty people, families, or just friends of my Dad who loved dirt bikes. By now my Dad had two bikes, having bought another one with a bigger engine. So the older one was now mine. I was slower than the others and totally terrified, but desperate for attention from my Dad. Doing guy things was the only way. One of the younger riders was a pretty skilled rider, equal to the best of the men. His size was suited to it, about average height for sixteen, but thin and quite polite, and excessively shy. His parents were friends with mine, but I actually had hardly spoken to him. Steve(B.) was the only boy I could think of to ask to my first school dance. He lived about an hour from us, so it was more than inconvenient, yet he agreed to go, perhaps with some parental pressure.

    To my best friend, Robin,going to any dance was a given. She always had a boyfriend who would take her. She was always dangerously ahead of me, socially. Her Mother could sew, so she made a simple long gown of lavender dotted swiss from a pattern for me and a similar one for Robin. We did our hair and makeup together, totally enthralled with the preparations, down to the boutonniere. Late on the afternoon of the dance, Steve arrived in his clean ugly car I didn't like, all polished up with a corsage for me. Our house was suburban awful, with dog pee on the curtains and bad furniture. But, I didn't know the difference. Off I took to the dance with my frail date. He started so wooden, as though he had never had a date and certainly only the most basic of instruction. He couldn't keep time on the dance floor and held my arms so stiffly. At the door I reached over to lightly kiss him on the mouth and say thank you. He shook so hard I wasn't sure of what was exiting out of the lower body. I felt bad for Steve. He sounded so embarrassed when I called to thank him for taking me. I didn't tell him it was my first date.

The next Steve (J.), was a tennis player, perhaps because his Dad was the Coach. I really had no idea how good he was. I was a dancer then, and despite never having played a sport, he took me to his Dad to ask if I had potential to play. Coach shook his head with eyes closed after the first five minutes. Steve was incredibly sweet to me. I asked him to the Sadie Hawkin's dance, an annual hay and costume event at school. Over the year, I would tell my Mom I was spending the night at Robin's after the usual Friday night events that school year and Robin and I would would meet at some friend's parent's house, parents away, of course, and enjoy the benefits of gallo wine hidden in the bushes waiting for our boyfriends to arrive. When they did, we would each claim a bedroom and hop in. Steve never pushed past making out. We got along fine till the summer arrived and time for the family annual three week camping trip. When we returned, my parents had a call from his Dad, the Coach, telling them he had gotten into heavy drugs while we were away and that I was a nice girl and should stay away from him. My best friend confirmed the story true from others that knew us. So he called me to come over in his VW van we had made out in. I could tell he was different, may have been high then. I had no experience with drugs, so I wouldn't have known. I said goodbye to him that warm starless night, knowing I was doing the right thing. He cried, but respected my decision. I heard later he spiraled into heroin.

A year later my Mom had had enough of my Father's philandering and demanded we move to their home town in Alabama. This was far greater seismic shift than the earthquakes we had grown accustomed to. My remainder lived to go to a windowless high school where my Dad was the new Principal. I blocked everything out for the next year and a half.

I met the next Steve (M.) summer after my freshman year at Alabama, a place I couldn't have dreamed up in California. I had decided to smoke during rush, which turned out didn't matter. I received a bid from one sorority anyway based on a letter someone who didn't know me wrote for my Dad. I turned it down, but pledged the Jewish sorority who had opened the door to us gentiles that year. I needed somewhere to belong. The first day I moved into the dorm with my Goodwill college crap, my roommate arrived to inform me in a serious tone as if preparing me for trial, that she lived with her boyfriend and what to say if her parents ever called. None of this worked for me.

    So I needed a job the summer after, while at the parental dwelling. A restaurant with a lively vibe had opened in our small north Alabama town. I cleaned up good and was assigned the job of hostess. My boss was Steve (M.), the assistant manager. I got to sleep late a lot, dress up and talk to people, and do very little. Turned out Steve's nickname was "Hollywood", he liked to wear printed shirts and was known for a sort of platform shoe, even though he was slightly over six feet tall. Guess he thought it made his ass look a little narrower. He was charming, handsome and sexy, so I started to see his unique shape as attractive to me. So we started going out. I didn't go back to school, terribly upsetting my parents. To compound their misery, I stayed out till 2 or 3 every night, then overnight at his place till my Dad said with disgust, "you're practically living with him". Steve wanted to open a restaurant, which I thought was very attractive, and he was from a prominent local family, which made him attractive, too. I liked the idea of finding a place, after being stranded for a year in Alabama. He had beautiful thick wavy brown hair and blue eyes. He wanted to be a businessman, the only way I saw out of the ball and chain of job keeping. I was hot for him, and desperate to get away from home. My parents gave the ultimatum, and sent me to Auburn to get me away from him. Steve went to work for restaurant group in their training program in Birmingham, and I drove there every weekend. I barely studied, barely went to class. It was like I was sex crazed. So we got married within a few months. I spent the next two years by myself as he worked the worst possible hours. He was promoted and transferred to Virginia, and I moved on to another retail position. We lasted there about a year, until one of the nearby restaurants was robbed at gunpoint. The next move for him was working construction supervision for a friend. They quarreled and he quit and decided to try finding himself in the great outdoors of Montana, alone. He was there for a couple of months without any thought of coming home. Home being my parent's converted garage. His former boss asked me in his absence, what had happened to him. "He really has no ambition", I told him, surprised at my candor. He returned home and went to a trade school, and life went along for another five or six years achingly slow and depressing. He got fat and spent his free time hunting, aspiring as he said "to be like the country people with true values". He insisted I not finish college, and contribute all the tips I made to the household fund. I remember standing on an intersection in the neighborhood I labeled going and nowhere, wondering what I had done, knowing I couldn't go back to my parents home for support, and realizing my idea of commitment, was total. So I shrunk his socks. And quite shockingly became pregnant. We called him Stevie, and he died in the hospital fighting inside me to stay. About six months after he was buried, Steve found a woman at work who did what women can do and became pregnant by him. He divorced me, married her with my ring, and named their child, Steve.

    I moved on and away and up and down the financial food chain. Then late in life through grace and luck fell really in love. I know I'm going to be ok now, because there's a Steve, but he lives across the street with his beer and third unhappy Peruvian wife. Some Steve is still in me though. My favorite curse word is still "fuck".

TINA BURNS

Supportive elementary school teachers always praised her writing, but it wasn't until Tina Burns was almost 50 years old that she took herself seriously – and she hasn't put the pen down since.

Tina has spent her career as a Human Resources manager with a local insurance firm, and returned to college to earn her BS in Communications from Kennesaw State University in 2010, graduating just three weeks before her 55th birthday!

She is married to a very supportive husband, Bruce Burns, and is the proud mother of three equally supportive sons: Tyler Windham, Jordan Windham, and Christopher Windham. Her family also includes an understanding dog named Ollie Beans.

Tina's writing style leans toward Humorous Memoir and Women's Fiction. While she had an agent for her first book, the work did not sell, but that hasn't dampened her enthusiasm for the craft. "I will get there someday!" she says.

All that is (Not) Holy
Excerpt from *The Ghost Chaser's Wife*

  Webb, my ghost-obsessed better half, and his spook troop minions head to Atlanta on a client requested investigation involving the presence of a wickedly large and obnoxious shadow. For those unfamiliar in the paranormal realm, shadow people are dark malevolent apparitions with no specific features. They have non-discernable faces and float about with the sole mission of scaring the crap out of anyone who sees them. Having never encountered a shadow entity, I do admit that I come from a long like of people who are afraid of their own shadows.
  Apparently, the shadow entity invading this family's domain has an affinity for their pet Beagle. The once housebroken pooch suffers from spontaneous fits of peeing, yelping, and humping. Sounds to me like a case of a good dog gone bad, and the anxiety-ridden family would be better served to fork over a few dollars and hire one of those infomercial people who could whisper calming affirmations into their pooch's ear. Problem solved.
  I waved off Webb's request that I participate in the shadow man pursuit by feigning stomach cramps. Truth be told, my intentions are to binge-watch episodes of *Wives With Knives* while gorging myself on leftover Christmas chocolate I bought on clearance last January, and hid in the freezer. In my 'hopped-up-on-tin-foiled-chocolate-Santas' state, I aim to solve every WWK within the first ten minutes of each episode, until I collapse into a sugar-induced coma. I envision Webb returning home to find me sprawled out on the living floor with a pile of uneaten Santas next to me, as I incoherently mumble from my

chocolate-frothed mouth that the blonde-haired bimbo with the big boobs is innocent.

A phone call from Webb interrupts my gorge fest - he left his holy water on the kitchen counter. Why am I not surprised? If he thinks I am peeling my butt off this sofa tonight, he better think again. "That sure sucks for ya', hon, but I gotta' go now. My tummy is rumbling something fierce. Be safe, love you, and buh-bye." The credits are rolling on the next case, and I can't afford to miss a single clue in the opening five minutes.

Webb resorts to pathetic pleading. "Tee, I left the house in a hurry and forgot the damn bottle. I need you to bring it to us."

"Webb, my stomach is giving me fits. I can't leave the house tonight." I unpeel and plop another miniature chocolate Santa into my mouth. "Don't your minions carry holy water on them? Or how about some of that banishing oil stuff? I'm sure there is a grocery store around there. You could jump in your van and run get some a lot quicker than I could drive all the way to Atlanta." Once again, problem solved.

Then Webb drops a doom bomb. "This is a worse case scenario here. Malevolent, intrusive – I'm worried for this family. I can't leave right now. I need you."

He just had to say those three little words – "I need you." What's a ghost chaser's wife to do?

I shove what's left of the chocolate Santas back into the freezer and commence turning the house upside down searching for the holy water. I see nothing that remotely resembles the blue bottle Webb always carries with him on investigations. I call Webb back to tell him to recheck his backpack.

"It's sitting on the kitchen counter next to the sink in a Perrier bottle. I scribbled the words 'holy water' on the label in black marker. You can't miss it."

Oh shit, damn, and hell! Did he say Perrier bottle? I poured that water down the sink during a commercial break an hour ago. I thought it was yet another 'empty' Webb left out. I firmly believe my husband has a genetic aversion to using our recycle bin.

"Babe, why are you keeping holy water in a Perrier bottle?" (insert distractive stall tactic while I decide whether I should tell him that his sacred holy water, previously destined to be splashed on the evil entity du jour, is now blessing the walls of our septic tank.)

"I didn't put it in the bottle, the minister who gave it to

me did," he replies.

"Why would a minister put holy water in a Perrier bottle?" (still stalling and still debating on whether to come clean.)

"Tee, I have no idea why the man put the holy water in a fucking Perrier bottle. Maybe he was fresh out of holy Tupperware containers. Enough with the twenty questions. I am past my ass and up to my eyeballs in hunting down shadows and getting dry-humped by a howling mutt. This is critical mode. Just grab the bottle and get your ass here." Critical mode is damn near close to being like a Homeland Security code orange. Webb and his team must be experiencing some nasty negative energy. Why else would he be so insistent that I drag my sick (lazy) body out of the house to get him that water?

"Webb, you shouldn't say fucking and holy water in the same sentence." My half-ass attempt to make him laugh fails miserably. I bet he's not even rolling his eyes at me. I assure him that I am out the door and on my way with the bottle of water. I just can't assure him what kind of water it is.

As I fish the empty Perrier bottle out of the recycle bin, I pain my brain trying to come up with someplace where I can score blessed water at this time of night.

Think, Tee. Where is the nearest Catholic Church? No, that won't work. Even if I find a church, any church, open this time of night, they aren't going to willingly donate a bottle of sacred water to some lunatic woman who claims her husband is holed up with a freaked-out family and their possessed dog. As I rinse some telltale Santa chocolate residue from my fingers, I see the obvious solution to my dilemma dripping from my hands - tap water! Webb will never know the difference. I hope. Another problem solved. I think.

As I drive to Atlanta, the green bottle of unholy water rolling around in the seat beside me, I begin to worry. While I doubt the existence of ghosts, spirits, or even shadow people, I do have a strong conviction about the evil of demonic entities. I thank my great-grandfather for this. As a child, my mother dragged me to summer tent revivals to hear Great Grandpa, a Pentecostal preacher, speak in tongues and cast out demons from those afflicted. He would slap the palm of his hand against the possessed person's forehead, and demand the devil leave this body. I sat quivering in a metal folding chair somewhere towards the back of the tent, wondering what happened to the deposed demons. Were they milling about the tent, looking for their next body to inhabit? I would pull my tiny legs up under my body and pray for the devil to pass me by.

I worry that the unblessed contents in the Perrier bottle won't keep a demon at bay. Without a second thought, I begin to pray. "Dear sweet Jesus, please don't let Webb kill me when he finds out I poured his holy water down the drain."

Then it occurred to me. Prayer is about changing things, right? And right now I need this tap water to miraculously change into holy water. I'm no priest, just the great-granddaughter of a Pentecostal evangelist - but desperate times, and all that shit. I pray the Lord's Prayer – the American Standard Version, of course, which specifically addresses that we be delivered from the 'evil one'. In this case, the 'evil one' could be Satan himself, disguised as a shadow man, or a horny Beagle.

I pull into the driveway of the investigation site and Webb leans in through the car window to retrieve the Perrier bottle. He plants a quick kiss on the top of my head, and insists that I join him in the house and meet the family and their dog. Plus, he wants me to be a part of the house blessing ritual, as I was so kind to deliver the necessary ingredient. Sure, why not? What do I have to lose? Either the imitation holy water banishes the evil, or it doesn't work and the house collapses into the sinkhole of hell, taking all of us plus the dog with it.

Webb updates me on tonight's investigation, relaying how two team members felt the presence of the shadow entity earlier, but were unable to capture photographic evidence. And the dog went for a romantic ride on his leg – twice. He cautions me, as he always does, not to ask the family if they 'really believe in this shit.' This man knows me too well.

My immediate impression is this is a nice family. The wife thanks me for making the drive out to their place at such a late hour and offers me a glass of tea. Their home is beyond gorgeous and has a media room the size of my entire house. Contrary to what the general population might think, most people who experience what they believe to be supernatural happenings in their home are not inbred, unemployed, uneducated single-wide trailer dwellers who think their velvet Elvis painting is haunted by the king, himself. The majority of Webb's private clients are hard-working, suburb-dwelling, highly intelligent, tax-paying members of society who just want confirmation of whatever is going on around them. Above all, they need someone to tell them that they are not bat-shit crazy.

As I take the glass of tea from the wife's trembling

hands, the family hound runs over to greet me. He begins sniffing my feet as if I'm a potential new two-legged girlfriend. As I balance the glass of tea in my right hand and attempt to thwart the dog's amorous advances with a nonchalant nudge to his private doggie parts using the toe of my left shoe, the wife starts describing the family's resident shadow. Let me tell you, it is difficult to focus on a conversation when you are dealing with a Beagle who thinks you are engaging in canine foreplay with him. The wife, lost deep within the sound of her own voice, continues her babbling, and I advance my defense strategies by interrupting her in mid sentence. "Excuse me. I think your dog needs a potty break." As she leads Cujo to the back door, I make my escape to the bathroom where I examine my shoes for damage, and vow to neuter that dog with my nail file if he comes within five feet of me again.

From my sanctuary in the bathroom, I hear Webb calling out for everyone to gather in the living room to begin blessing the house. I take a surveillance position and hang back from the group to enjoy the free show. Webb has other plans for me, and drags me over next to him like a disobedient child who must be kept under tight control - his discrete way of telling me to keep my eyes and ears open and my big mouth shut. I flashback to the tent revivals of my youth, and want to curl up to protect myself from whatever is about to be dejected from this home. I also want to protect my legs in case Romeo the horn dog singles me out in the crowd.

Webb and the other investigators recite a short prayer of protection to Saint Michael. They walk from room to room, repeating the prayer as Webb pours the holy water into his hand and sprinkles it about. I recite my own prayer of protection in case a random bolt of lightning strikes me for pissing off a demon for dousing him with ordinary tap water.

The blessing completed, Webb asks that we join hands and recite the Lord's Prayer. I bow my head, keeping one eye open to watch for the possible shadowy wrath. Prayer over, Amen. Can we go home now? Uh, apparently not, as there is the matter of the yelping horny Beagle parked under a coffee table licking his male bits. With the family's permission, Webb approaches the dog, offers a prayer and a blessing, before splashing a generous portion of holy water onto the mutt. As if someone blasted him with the jet spray of a water hose, the dog lets out a surprised cry, tucks his tail between his legs, and hauls ass out from under the table.

A quiet collective sigh hangs in the air. The nice family appears to be at a state of peace. The wrinkled lines of worry in their collective faces disappear. Even the dog resigns from his howling and humping to stretch out by the back door. 'Good-byes' and words of thanks are exchanged as the team packs up their equipment. Webb passes out confirmational hugs to the family and tells them to call should they need his help in the future. He instructs them how to repeat the blessings and where to obtain holy water, if needed. I bite my tongue and head for my car.

The next morning over breakfast, Webb cannot stop talking about the previous night's investigation. Our conversation drifts to the power of faith, or blind faith, as I think of it. Did the holy water and prayer rid that home of evil? Or was it pure unadulterated faith that removed the family's fear? Whatever the answer is, I am proud Webb played a role in helping that family, even if he did surrender his dignity to the dog – twice.

I'm convinced Webb would make a good minister. Strong in his unwavering faith, people flock to him like he's this giant-ass magnet of reassurance. He has that certain charisma about him - the right mix of sincerity and humility. He reminds me of my great-grandfather. Two men, spiritually strong, who want to rid the world evil, one demon at a time. Only Webb doesn't cruise around a tent, talking gibberish, and slapping people upside the head.

All this kitchen table talk about faith makes me feel a bit guilty about my holy water cover-up. Before I can stop myself, I blurt out, "Webb, there is something I need to tell you about the water in that Perrier bottle." He looks at me as if he knows what I am about to confess.

"You took a swig of it to see what it tastes like, didn't you?" That loud 'thunk' is the sound of my jaw hitting the table. "Well, I have to tell you that I'm guilty of doing the same thing a few years back. Don't worry about it. It's only filtered tap water that somebody with a ton of faith prayed over."

Amen, Webb, Amen.

Night Writers

We kindred spirits who must write
    Words in the night
Abandon our lovers
    Or others
While we pass time
    Immortalizing our minds
Dreaming of what could have been
    With a stroke of our pen
Lonely angels we become
    Psalms roll from our tongues
Of passion and pain and nonsense
    Of truth and pretense
In due time all awake
    To the gifts we create
Listen…and read…and know
    The words we bestow
Took wing from nocturnal flight
    We weavers of words in the night

Traffic and Rain

The view from the big picture window in their living room was no different today than any other day at this hour. The afternoon traffic snaked along the two-lane road that ran just past their house. It would only be a short time before they would join in the traffic and make the four-minute drive that recent events deemed necessary. The September rain fell gently but steadily, forcing drivers to turn on the headlights to their cars. She paced back and forth in front of the picture window, sometimes staring inward at him and sometimes staring outward at the traffic. She always dreaded going out in the rain this time of day and hoped it would stop before they had to leave the house to make their short trip. He sat in his recliner with the small dog in his lap. He fidgeted with the remote to the television, never turning the set on.

"That's odd. There's a rainbow in the west but it's still raining. Isn't that strange?" she waited for his reply.

"It's not that strange. It's probably off in the distance, where it's not raining. Nothing unusual about that."

"I'm going to put on a pot of coffee. Will you drink a cup if I do?" she called out to him as she crossed the living room into the kitchen.

"Only if you make decaf, or I'll be up all night," he responded.

"What makes you think you will be able to sleep tonight?" she asked, but in a tone so low he never heard her question.

As the coffee brewed, she opened the cupboard and took

out the souvenir mugs from the Tybee Island Lighthouse she bought on their vacation the previous June. Her hands trembled slightly.

"Is the traffic still heavy?" she called out to him from the kitchen.

"Is it still raining?" she added.

"I don't know. I'm not sitting where I can see out the window. But from the sound of it hitting the roof, I can tell it's still raining. Maybe not as heavy as earlier, but it is still raining."

In a few moments she returned to the living room with the two mugs of coffee. She sat his mug on the table by his side and tried to offer a smile. It was not returned.

"You'll have to put the dog down to drink your coffee. You might spill it on her, and it's pretty hot. She might get burned."

"I think I know not to juggle a small dog and a mug of coffee at the same time" he retorted as he eased the dog onto the floor beside him.

"It's almost four o'clock. We have to be there by four thirty, did you say?" she looked up at the clock on the mantle then over to him.

"Yes, four thirty. I've told you this several times before. We have to be there by four thirty because they close at five o'clock."

"Did I get your coffee right? Enough sugar?"

"Yes, it's fine. Thanks."

"In another hour this will all be over with," she said to him.

"Let's not get into a discussion about this, okay?"

"Well, then what do you suggest we discuss? The weather? I've already told you it's raining and there is a rainbow. I don't know whether I find the rainbow symbolic or ironic." She shrugged her shoulders and bowed her head.

"Obviously you need some kind of reassurance about this whole thing. It's very simple, really. No more than a couple of minutes and it's over with."

She looked at him then away from him and gazed out the window at the traffic. It was almost at a standstill.

"I will stay there the entire time. Everything is going to be all right. You will see," he said to her.

"And what about afterward? Will everything be all right afterward? Will we be all right afterward? I'm almost falling apart now. What will I be like an hour from now?"

"We will be fine."

"You really are sure about this?" she moved closer to him.

"I think it's for the best. I think you will see that as well. But if you don't want to do it, then we won't."

"I just don't like the idea of playing God" she said to him.

"We waited for God to make a decision and it didn't happen. Now we have to. Do you have some sort of religious conflict about this? If so, you've waited until the last possible moment to bring it up. Well?" he looked her square in the eye when he asked.

"I just don't want to play God. I feel like I, rather we, are playing God."

"Then that's it. We won't go through with this - end of discussion. I would never ask you to do something you don't feel right about. It's obvious that you just don't want to do this."

She focused her eyes straight into his and replied, "Once we do this we can't take it back. We will never be the same. We will be 'us', but not the same 'us'. Not the 'us' that we are this very instant before we go playing God. Will we question this decision? This decision to play God?"

He looked at her and repeated, "This is for the best. You must know that. How can you not know that?"

"I do know that," she replied. "I just don't want to accept it. But I will, for you. I will play God just this once and accept this just for you."

"Don't put it on me that way. This has to be unanimous. I am not going to allow you to say that this was my doing – my decision. I will call this off before I allow that."

"Do you want to call it off? Is that what you are suggesting?"

"No, I am just stating that I will call it off if it's not what you genuinely feel is for the best" he replied.

Outside the traffic snake had ceased to crawl along the road. There was only the occasional car passing by. He slowly rose from his chair and put down the souvenir mug with the lighthouse on it. He walked over to the picture window where she stood. He rubbed her left shoulder with his right palm, as he had always done in moments of tension between them. She released a soft sigh.

"The rainbow is gone," she said then continued, "I'm trying so hard to be brave and not cry. I do know it's what must be done."

"Look, I promise I will stay right there and it will be over with quickly. A couple of needle sticks and she will go right to sleep. She won't feel a thing. It will be so much easier on her this way. Don't you really want what's best for her?"

"Are we going to bring her back home?" she asked.

"We will do whatever you wish, whatever you feel is best."

As she scooped up the little dog in her arms and prepared to head for the car he asked her one last time, "Are you sure you're okay with this?"

"I am fine. It's all fine and okay. Please don't ask me that again. Please don't make me answer that question again."

He didn't speak for a moment, but then said to her, "It's still raining. I'll get a blanket to wrap her in."

DEBBIE HOUSE

The very first story Debbie House wrote was about a mouse in a space ship. Her teacher wrote "Delightful" under the A+ grade, and Debbie was thrilled. She was in the 4th grade.

Debbie recently retired from 32 years in customer service. Her career has also included pre-school teacher, medical assistant, and animal rescue volunteer for causes. (She is also a Licensed Pesticide Applicator; "The test was very difficult.")

Her favorite job has been being a mom to her son, Dusty, who is 35 and married to a beautiful girl named Heather.

Debbie has been married to her husband, David - "a kind & patient man" - for 13 years. She also is close to her younger brother, Billy, and to her 81-year-old mother, who is "quite frisky, and shares her opinions openly."

Debbie hopes to gain the confidence to write about the things that she has scribbled on the backs of grocery receipts "and various other surfaces when ideas come to me at unexpected times."

Animal Medicine

"Believe it brothers and sisters! Do not allow the devil to take over your thoughts. When you think unclean thoughts, when you covet your neighbor's wife, you are bound for hell. Come to church every Sunday. If you are not here on Sunday, you open the door to the devil." Preacher Wilkie wiped the sweat off his forehead with a fresh white handkerchief and took a long sip of water.

He started up again, seeming fully renewed and energized. He held his bible in his left hand and slapped on it with his right, *slap, slap*. "While Sister Ellen sings, won't you come?" He rocked back and forth on his heels and shouted "Someone under the sound of my voice is not saved. I sense the devil in this very room with us right now. This is your invitation to come down and pray for your salvation. Won't you come? If you are not saved, you will spend eternity in misery with the devil."

Sister Ellen was singing "Just As I Am "as if she didn't get a wink of sleep Saturday night. I had never seen anybody sing while yawning before. I whispered to Gran to look at her and she told me to be quiet.

Eddie Long sprang from his seat and ran down to the front. "Preacher Wilkie, I'm saved, you all know that I am a man of God, but I just want to testify that since I found Jesus, my whole life has changed. If you don't know the Lord, please come down. I will pray with you. "

Well, we all had to wait until Laney Westbrook went down and was saved 45 minutes later. It was a wonderful day for all the good people of Morgan Springs First Baptist Church. They had prayed hard and saved souls. Tears were shed and it was way past lunch time.

I was 9 years old and terrified that I had been in the same

room as the devil. Not only that, but if I don't find and get to know Jesus, I will be a crispy critter for all eternity. I asked mom and Gran if they knew Jesus and mama told me that I must love Jesus more than anything. I asked her, "Even more than you, mama?" She looked very serious and said "Someday you will understand, Elizabeth. " I was more baffled than ever. Why should I listen to a preacher who has plastic flowers at the entrance of his church?

Later that same week, I was explaining to my daddy that I was really worried about the devil and Jesus and not being right with the Lord. He called Preacher Wilkie in the middle of the night and told him to get over to our house. He prayed with me for what seemed like hours, coaching me with the words to ask Jesus to save me. I finally rose and said with great enthusiasm "I've been saved!"

Preacher Wilkie smiled and praised the Lord with his hands raised up toward heaven. Lizzie Swanson had become a child of God.

I looked over at my brother and he gave me a look of relief and doubt at the same time. He was already saved since he was a Mr. Know-It-All.

I crawled into bed that night not feeling one single bit better because I knew nothing had changed. The great heart-pounding, soul-cleansing spiritual experience had not really taken place at all. I just wanted it to stop. My dog, Sweetie, curled up next to me and put her head on my chest as if to say everything will be alright. Sleep came soon after.

Summer was always perfect at Gran's. We would sit in the yard in the evening with my cousins and aunts and shuck corn and snap beans. We talked about everything.

One night, there was a man's voice that got louder and louder down the road. He was yelling. We listened and he kept on, but we couldn't make sense of his words. My brother was worried and said "what's wrong?"

"Don't worry, Ben. It's Ned Lott. He's just shouting." Uncle Eb nodded at Ben to ease his mind.

"About what?"

"Shouting to the Lord. He goes up the hill behind his house sometimes to praise the Lord."

The grown-ups talked about God. I felt the conflict in my heart again.

###

Gran and I would walk through the woods often. Spring and Summer especially. She would point out and name the various plants and trees to me. She would tell me about making tea from Sassafras and how the oil from Birch tree leaves makes a good tonic for gout and kidney stones.

"God gave us the trees and plants to use as medicines and for our enjoyment. In return, it is our job to care for them and all of the Earth." Gran looked at me as if she wanted me to promise to do just that.

"I solemnly swear to love the Earth, Gran. "

"Lord knows your Mama can't be trusted with it." Gran laughed. "She kills everything."

"She lets me have my animals and they are part of creation, Gran." I defended Mama, even though Gran was just having fun. I thought of my cat, my dogs and all of the animals. I felt grateful for the Earth and all of creation.

I'm told that I was born a sensitive person. That might explain why it hurt my feelings when my daddy went out to buy a new truck and never came back. We were going to the fair just as soon as he got home.

We ate a lot of Chef Boyardee Ravioli for a while. Brother Ben was happy, but I got sick of it.

Then we moved in with Gran. Life at Gran's was nice. Her house always smelled good, like strawberry cobbler and cornbread.

The only just awful thing was Gran loved church, so we always had to go. Mama had a job at Foodland so she didn't have to go. I so wished that I was old enough to get a job at Foodland. No church and Daniel worked there. He had long hair and was very handsome and rebellious looking.

One Sunday, Mavis Haney shared a vision she had when the Lord spoke to her. She said when she prayed the Lord always answered her prayers. She confessed it was because she lived to do the Lord's work. Then Deacon Crandall told us how the Lord had cured him of a bout of diarrhea that had been hanging onto him for 3 weeks. It's a miracle!

I had been on my knees praying for my daddy to come home. It never happened and the Lord didn't say La-Dee-Da to me!

Gran and I were on our walk in the woods one afternoon and lo and behold, Mavis Haney was butt naked and laid out a quilt over a patch of Virginia creeper doing something that looked unnatural with Preacher Wilkie. I rubbed my eyes wondering if I was having a vision. Nope.

Gran and I made it home in record time and I somehow knew, probably because of that sensitivity thing, not to ask questions. I wondered, but kept it to myself, if Mavis and Preacher Wilkie were doing the Lord's work. Probably not.

###

Gran was very sick one winter. We prayed and asked everyone in town to pray for her. She had a disease in her lungs. It was really hard to see her suffer like that. A lot of people came to visit and it just seemed to make her more tired. Before I would go to bed each night, I would look to see if Gran was breathing. I had overheard one of the ladies in the choir say to Mama, "I'm afraid Sally is not going to make it." Mama sent her packing and shouted as the screen door slammed, "You are not welcome here!"

Poor Gran died. The Earth shifted in mourning. The sun didn't come out for days. That's how I remember it.

At Gran's funeral, Preacher Wilkie spewed about how Sally Walton was not gone, but in her heavenly home. She is living in a mansion on a street paved with gold.

I experienced a true ass-chapping with Preacher Wilkie and his kind. As for the Lord, I didn't know him and he didn't know me.

Mama went downhill, too. She had lost daddy and now Gran. After a while, she took up dancing and dating. I was glad to see her out in the world again. She was beautiful and deserved to be happy.

Ben got his driver's license and had this uncanny ability to have fun and friends everywhere, all the time.

Two weeks after high school graduation, I moved to Atlanta.

The first night there, per Mama's instructions, I ate Krystal hamburgers and went to the Toddle House for cheesecake. I loved Atlanta.

Thanks to Uncle Eb, I had an interview at the *Atlanta Journal-Constitution*. I wanted to be a writer, but they hired me to sell advertising. It was hard work but I learned a lot. I was there three years before they gave me a shot at writing.

Sometimes I wanted to be a kid in the country again. I saw hungry and homeless people and stray dogs and cats with nowhere to go. Working at the paper, I heard all of the news. So much suffering. As Gran would have said, there is not enough love in the world.

One Saturday afternoon, on my walk, my mind was quiet. I took a second to acknowledge that my meditation class was paying off. I noticed how very beautiful the grass was, how kudzu smells like grape Kool-Aid when in bloom. The breeze was wonderful. The sun was perfect.

My new friend, an appaloosa, a grey dapple amazing creature of perfect beauty, approached the fence to greet me. This was a ritual now. I rubbed his nose and gave him a carrot. I really must meet the parents of this beautiful animal to learn his name, I thought. He nuzzled me. I love him. I pressed down the middle and raised up the top of the barbed-wire fence and stepped in.

Always a cautious person, I wondered for a moment if the owners would mind my trespassing on their property and feeding their horse without their permission. I sat down on the grass while my friend finished his treat.

He gently neighed and lowered his head. I rose to my knees and pressed my face against his. The sun was going down, but there was no way I was going to leave this spot. That baby lay down beside me. I moved as closely to him as I could and stroked this beautiful animal until tears of joy flooded my face. I let my head fall softly against him and just let the tears flow.

I realized that night how often animals and I had found each other, how often I had turned to them and they to me. How many people do you know that have held chickens in their laps like kittens? I feel spiritual when I am in the presence of animals.

Suddenly, my mind became a slideshow of all the animals in my life since my childhood. The love and magic I felt, I KNEW when I was with them. They had mended my broken heart and eased my pain many times.

Maybe because I could never reconcile the Lord God as described by a country preacher, I came to know and understand unconditional love from these beautiful creatures whose presence was and always will be sacred to me. After all, they are part of the creation I promised Gran I would care for.

I don't try to define God anymore. I don't attempt to make sense of the Old Testament or the Virgin Birth. I just see the creator in nature, on my walks, in every animal I meet and of course, in me.

Amen. And so it is.

ELISE NOELLE

Science Fiction writer Elise Noelle is a senior at Veritas High School, whose first piece of writing was "a novel I wrote ages ago... that will never see the light of day."

Completing a novel was a major accomplishment, and she has been writing ever since. Over the course of several years, she has researched and written a Sci-Fi trilogy, for which she is currently seeking representation.

Elise lives with her mum and father, and many animals, including her three cats, Tessie, Yargo, and Piper.

In addition to her career as an author, Elise looks forward to attending Berry College next fall, to pursue her degree in Psychology.

A Soul Is But Stories

"Terian?"
Although his mood before was far from joy, now it was tense. Almost as if there were more bad news. Though I doubted that, Life had lost the ability of the worse.

He shook his head, already knowing my question. Tossing his blood stained coat on the chair, he sat down on the edge of the bed. "Are you alright?" His tone was edged, though it wasn't the anger or remorse I was so accustomed to hearing from him. It was edged with...

I nodded, trying to focus. "I'm alright." The word, however, was only suiting to how I had been. I still could barely walk and my thoughts...they were worse. I couldn't...think. Even trying to hold on to a conversation was arduous. My own thoughts were becoming impossible, unfathomable things. However, my body, though I felt sick, no longer felt hand in hand with death. Now, it was only lingering in the door.

Terian's eyes flashed silver, again with that unnamed emotion. "Is it worse?" His voice was no longer glass and water; the glass had shattered.

Fear, that was the emotion I was looking for. It was same thing I was overcome with...last night? Could it be last night? Only last night? It felt like a century ago, and I was no longer certain if that distance, the haze I was in, was from my own choking emotions or if it was from the disease. I could no longer till the two apart.

"Aviah?" he asked, meeting my eyes, taking my hand. For a moment I forgot we were speaking of anything at all.

I shook my head, trying to focus, to wake up from the darkening fog I was trapped in. "I'm not worse not before." Physically it had helped. The rest, however, were lies.

However, either Terian had already guessed the truth or I could no longer spin a lie because again that flicker of emotion lit his eyes. I still could not find its name; the only comparison I could give to it was…

Was….what was I thinking?

Where was I?

There were noises and words and a sea of senses, but I recognised not one of them. Not this place with the red walls nor the curtains hanging like dead men on their hooks nor the shadows painting across of the room of darkness. Not even the pale sheets triggered a memory of the familiar. None of it I knew, none of it I recognised, especially not the man in front of me with the jade-green eyes.

He looked as haunted and as pained as the room. His clothing was stained the same red coating the walls. And with those shifting shadows casting along his cheek bones and his pale blonde hair, he looked like a spectre. Like a tortured soul. Like how one would have imagined Heathcliff leaning against the tree outside of his beloved's home, the home that now housed her stone cold body. Or the sinner in Ellard's novel looking upon the world, knowing with a heavy heart the choices he had.

Such imagines of these were coloured with each stroke of despair, devastation, and death, these were the imagines of the man with the jade-green eyes.

"Who are you?" I asked, yanking my hand back from him. I didn't know him. I didn't know any of this.

The depiction of before shattered.

"Aviah," he said with a voice that reminded me of broken glass. However, whatever words he was planning on speaking vanished along with the display of his emotions. It was like a painting scrubbed clean. "I'm not going to hurt you."

I narrowed my eyes, looking him over again. "Why? Why do you say that?"

"Because, love, that's the truest answer I can give you," he told me, meeting my eyes. I saw now that there was silver in those green eyes. "Anything else will either be a water down half-truth or dogged lie."

"Then why should I believe it at all?" I challenged.

"Do you remember anything?" he asked instead, skipping over my question.

I glared, not appreciating his lack of a response. However, my glower faded once I realised the answer to his question. It wasn't a no...yet it was far from a yes. It was like the memories and everything else were indeed there...but it was hazed. Like frozen water, I could no longer see under the surface.

I frowned. I felt as if I too were frozen like my memories. Ice was all there was left. I didn't, couldn't respond, glancing away. My eyes went back to the corners of the room as if the darkness held some answer, some solace.

"Aviah," he said again. The emotion was back in his voice, beautiful and pained. "Will you let me explain?"

I looked back up, meeting his gaze. "I can't trust you."

"I know," he said. "Although, I doubt you would be in a room with me, love, if it wasn't of your free will."

He did have a point, I thought. And by making that statement, knowing me well enough to, I must have had something to do with him. Moreover, I didn't have any other way to find out information. I didn't even know where this room was.

"Alright," I said. "Then tell me why I'm here."

"You were, are sick. We're travelling to Germany to see if we can find treatment that would cure you." Although he was doing his best to stifle his emotions, his voice was still lanced with tension.

"Sick," I repeated. "From what?"

He ran a hand through his hair. "AIDs. It's a viral disease."

I frowned again. The word AIDs meant nothing to

me. I understood what a virus was, and I did feel sick. I felt like I was both freezing and burning, as if my body could not bring itself to decide its temperature. Even my bones felt worn and I knew, without doubt, they were beyond my control. So I didn't disagree I was sick, but what did that have to do with my memory?

Although I wanted to know the answer, that wasn't what I asked.

"And what are we?" Enemies? Friends? He knew me. However, merely knowing and the emotion behind that knowledge were two different things. How did he know me? As a friend? Not that I had friends, I thought. An enemy? He acted far too concerned for that, unless he was lying.

My question was like a pin falling in an empty room. There was the sound of the words but there was not a sound to follow. No response. No movement. The only noise that remained was the beating of a heart, the whistle of the wind, and the booming noise of silence.

"Well?" I asked again. "What are we?"

When he met my eyes, he said only, "Do you want the truth or the short answer?" His voice was still neutral as if the conversation was of no more importance than the weather. However, underneath his tone were the depths of sorrow hidden as only a slight edge of his intonation.

I raised a brow. "You did say you knew me."

I shouldn't be so cruel, I thought, but I had to know. This won't haunt him so if I were simply a passing friend. So, I didn't want the easy spoken lie, even if the truth was arduous. Not that I thought the truth would somehow help me or give me an advantage. It was most likely the worst thing I could hear. However, I needed to know.

And, after all, I was already trapped in a room with a man I did not remember. How much worse could it get?

"We are, were," he corrected. "Married."

The dead silence from before was back with a vengeance, a corpse leering over the room. I no longer heard the heart beating or the whistle of the wind- not even the looming of the twice fallen silence.

The only thing I did hear and heard over and over like the tune of dying screams was that word. Married.

Although I didn't remember, I couldn't believe it. I hadn't- wouldn't, have simply fallen in love and gotten married. I knew the term, even without my memories, and I felt the dust of its obsoleteness. To resurrect such a thing would not have been done so flippantly nor would he lie about it. It was not the sort of thing one used in their spinning of lies. It was unbelievable. Which meant, I thought, he was telling the truth.

And such a truth...I shook my head. I had loved him? I thought, glancing back at him. No, that wasn't possible, not for me. I was without memories; however, this truth had always been indwelled in me, in my bones, in my soul.

I could not love. That was impossible.

"Love-"

I recoiled from his word and such a word it was.

"*Stop.*"

I hadn't realised I yelled until I saw his expression.

He, with those pale jade-green eyes, appeared to be immortal. As if, I thought, he had seen every horror, every broken sorrow, every fall of every empire. But that too was not possible.

"I'm sorry," I said, glancing away from his gaze before changing the subject. "What did you say your name is?"

It wasn't the question I should be asking; however, I didn't know what else to say. What words could I give to the stranger? While he may know me, I knew nothing, not of him, not of anyone. My mind was a frozen lake waiting for a summer that would never come.

"Terian," he replied. Somehow he kept up the same tone, a blank tone without emotion except for that edge...

He was liar, I thought, to be able to keep such a perfect act. I imagined, if we were married, what Hell this must be for him for he remembered everything.

How long, I wondered, had I forgotten? Was this merely a replay of events I could not remember? Where was the line between forgetting and not existing?

However, I did not ask this. Maybe I didn't want to know, and, in a way, it did not matter. So, instead, I asked. "Why didn't you leave?"

Like the truth of knowing I could not love, I knew, as much as I knew the words I spoke, that I could not be loved- not unconditionally. Sooner or later, this broken tune would wear and become an old, worthless thing. All humans eventually became tired of that same old, terrible thing.

"Aviah," Terian said. His tone suddenly sparked, like lightning striking a forest, sudden, bright, and furious. "Don't. I don't give a *damn* if you hate me. However, don't you dare believe that for a bloody moment. You are the most important thing left on this damned, rotting earth to me." His eyes were silver.

"Do you read minds too?" My tone was cold, not of anger, but shock. Shock by his emotions, by his words, by the impossible.

Although, the scene, the words felt familiar, I thought, the emotion was still lingered there. And much like the sleep walker waking from a dream, I couldn't not remember the details. All I had was shock and reminiscence.

He shook his head, a ghost of a distant smile on his lips. "No, though, I am glad to see that hasn't changed."

"What hasn't changed?" My words coming out too fast before I realised the cruelty of what I was saying. Was that who I was? Cruel? Heartless?

"Your snark."

"You mean my malice?" I corrected.

"You weren't cruel. I just happen to know," he said, reaching to move back my hair that had fallen forward before he stopped himself, quickly taking his hand back. "How to get under your skin," he finished. His smile had faded along with his words when he had pulled his hand back. It had obviously been a habit for him to carelessly touch me, and the way he spoke those words, I imagined he was intimately familiar with 'getting under my skin.'

His expression changed again, apparently 'reading my thoughts.'

"Don't go there," I told him.

This time, with that line, the words almost gave away to the melting of the frozen ice of the lake. But the ice remained as thick as ever and all I had was an off kilter sense of Deja vu.

He, almost, grinned. "Why not, love?"

I glared, about to retort, before losing my train of thought. Wasn't something supposed to happen here?

I shook my head as if that would stop the nagging feeling of scattered, unremembered memories. "Will I ever remember again?" I asked, although, I hadn't meant to say those words, let alone think them. Not when, I thought, the answer was quite so apparent.

"You'll most likely remember briefly," Terian stopped, deciding to rephrase his words. "Before a treatment we used is exhausted from your body."

My eyes narrowed. "Treatment?" I repeated. The "briefly" was no more than a cold polite way of saying that I would exist between clarity and chaos until the haze conquered what little I had left. His allusion of *treatment*, however, was nothing more than a word chosen to avoid 'upsetting,' me.

He opened his mouth to reply. I stopped him before he even started. "I want the truth." Well, maybe not wanted, but I did need it.

"We're genetically modified soldiers," he told me. As if that were enough of an explanation.

"Which means?"

Whatever he was dancing around was something he thought I wasn't going to like. Though, that description wasn't quite right. He was, and had been, treating me like I was fragile, as if one word, one thing, one action would set me off. That was why he was so careful answering my questions, so hesitant to even touch me.

Why did he expect me to break? Had I before?

"We're stronger, faster than humans and have enhanced senses," he answered, pausing just slightly before continuing. "And we have to consume blood to survive."

"That doesn't tell me anything about my question." The reply he did give was surreal, but I had no memories to tell me if that was normal or not. Maybe it was;

however, that wasn't as important as the 'treatment.' Which, I thought, hadn't work, seeing as I was still in this condition.

But I would be willing to try again, or anything else for that matter, if only I could remember, to think lucidly.

"You took my blood."

I frowned. "Why?" That wasn't the reply I was expecting.

"The virus you have effects the body's T cells. You aren't able to consume human blood because your T cells can no longer transfer foreign blood to your own," Terian explained.

"What does that have to do with the treatment?" I was still sick, still lost.

"It brought you time." His voice was damaged again like he remembered some terrible thing, and I knew what it was. Of course I did. It was the same horrendous thing that stayed, lurking for the chance to sink its fangs into the heart of man.

Death.

"How much?" How much longer until I died? To leave a life I didn't remember living. A life I lost, a life I never had.

"A little less than two weeks," he said.

Two weeks of forgetting, of fading then, I thought.

I was already dead.

Although I couldn't decide which was worse: for me to lose an unremembered, unburden life or for him to live a remembered, broken life.

Were the memories he had worth the torture? Was I lucky to fade to nothing?

I didn't know the answer, for I knew nothing of the world I was leaving. But if I was the lucky one, then why was my heart breaking?

Lost in the thoughts, the questions, and the haze of my own mind, I hadn't noticed that Terian had stood. His blood stained coat was back on, clearly intending on leaving. "I'll see you next evening." Simple words- like the conversation of death never happened. He mistook my silence for needing space.

Quite frankly, I thought, that was the last thing in the

world I wanted. I couldn't bear to be left alone to questions I could not answers and thoughts I could not have.

So words I would never dare say fell from my lips. "Can you stay?"

Terian stopped, the door between us already open. Surprise briefly flickered across his face before he shoved it away. "Of course," he said, pausing, "Unless- do you want me to?"

"Unless you have somewhere you need to go?" I was not being weak.

He raised a brow. "Even if I did," he said, sitting back down next to me, "I won't leave you. Of course, that's until you throw me out."

"Did I do that before?" I asked. I wondered how we managed to get married if we fought so often.

"No, although, there is always a first, love," he said, half grinning.

I was going to ask something else before I shivered, the cold I had been ignoring finally getting the better of me. I only wished I could blame it on the surroundings; however, the cold was in my bones, haunting and freezing me like a ghost in my veins.

"Love," Terian said, seeing my shudder before I could hide it. "Do you mind if I...?"

"It alright," I allowed. I trusted him more or less, and even if I didn't, it wasn't as if he could kill me. I was already dying. Perhaps that was immortality, I thought.

He moved, pulling me into his arms. It was closer than I would have liked, though I couldn't complain. He was burning, like standing too close to a flame. "Better?" He asked.

I nodded before asking. "How are you so warm?" Surely I wasn't that freezing, I thought.

"Electricity," he replied simply before concern dripped into his voice. "Is it too hot?"

I ignored his vague 'answer;' I wasn't going to go anywhere with asking him about that. "Why do you keep treating me like I'm delicate?"

Terian raised both brows. "I never said you were, love."

"No, but your acting like it," I pointed out.

He sighed. "The truth? I'm expecting Hell to become worse."

"Meaning, Terian?" I didn't know how I kept patience with him before.

"Meaning," he said. "I'm expecting a lapse, a hallucination, some fitting twist of fate."

I raised a brow. "I hallucinated before?"

He nodded and before I could ask, he said. "The hallucinations were memories, distorted memoires." Judging by his tone, I doubted they were pleasant memories without the distortion.

Was my life that horrific? Was it worth fighting?

I shook my head again, trying to clear it, to rid myself of the never ending plague of questions. They would go nowhere, and although Terian had not mentioned, I was right. I would keep forgetting. This moment, the small answers I had, the fear and the hope, all of it I would forget. Every breath, every second was of a life I had already lost.

I was nothing more than breathing heap of flesh.

No, as much as despised it, my questions, my hope, they were pointless. Even if I managed a miniscule step towards a solution, I would forget. I would always be reclaimed to the haze that had taken root in my mind. It had already wiped away my memories; it would only be a matter of time before it swept me away with it. After all, I was already dead.

For a soul is but stories, and I had no more stories to tell.

"Would it help to sleep?" Terian asked, breaking apart my thoughts. Although, seeing the torn expression on his face, he, no doubt, knew what those thoughts were.

I shook my head. "I don't think I can." Although I wouldn't mind an escape from the ruins inside my head.

"I can use an electric pulse," he said. Gone was the fury and passion of before, gone was the nostalgia, gone was the thread of hope. Instead, Terian was once more the strange and tortured man.

I'm sorry, I thought, not saying the words out loud.

Somehow, I knew he wouldn't appreciate them. So, instead, I nodded, taking his hand. It was the best I could give with words or an argument.

    The rest faded to nothing.

CHERYL TAYLOR

Creative people often tend to bring their vision to many areas of their lives, and Cheryl Taylor is living proof.

Born and raised in Great Britain, Cheryl pursued Business Studies at St. Albans College ("I hated it."), then fashioned her career as an Advertising Media Planner Buyer, Fashion Designer, and manufacturer specialising in wedding gowns – although she also lent her talents to sportswear, children's special occasion wear, and high-end dolls.

An English Emigre, Cheryl and her husband, Carl, moved from St. Albans – near London – with their two daughters, Rosie and Catie. Their son, Adam, arrived a few years later. Six years ago, they became American citizens.

Cheryl enjoys reading and writing in a variety of genres. Her first taste of writing for an audience was providing fashion tips for magazines and newspapers in England. She began taking Creative Writing classes at FoxTale Book Shoppe two years ago, and found that she really enjoys telling stories. She said she intends to write a lot, and maybe even finish a book or two!

Tell It To the Crows

At the day's end, when the late sun shines warm and hazy, as the heat ripples the atmosphere, Chalcy runs through the long grass. Chalcy appears blurred against the pale yellowy, blue sky, her body indistinct, almost merging into the horizon. Running, running, running, her pace urgent, heels thrust high behind her then plunge forward, soles slapping hard onto dusty soil. Chalcy's determined momentum forcing her forward.

"What are you running from?" Asks Grandma.

Chalcy's desperate pace comes to an abrupt halt, her face flushed, chest heaving, wild, un-tamed hair urgently swept back from her sweaty brow by hot clammy hands.

"I've got to tell them crows something." Chalcy's pale blue eyes peer at the black crows perched high up in the huge oak tree.

Grandma nods agreement, her right hand pats the child's hot head.

"Go right ahead, be my guest. Shall we sit? "

Chalcy shakes her head and runs into the shade of the tree. Chalcy thrusts her hands skyward, and commences her indignant rant, venting all the pent up anger, frustration and injustices committed against her by the local bullies.

An opera of cawing crows peck at Chalcy's morsels of dialogue. She shares with them all her pain and sadness and the crows gobble it all up. With every ingested word their raven feathers darken, enhanced and evermore beautiful.

Chalcy finishes her diatribe, the crows cock their heads, awaiting her next move. Exhausted she collapses to the ground, legs criss-cross apple sauce her upturned palms rest upon her knees, eyes closed, she slows her breath. Grandma sits and joins her in meditation.

The crows listen, intelligent beady eyes, alert yet still, beaks silent, feathers polished and iridescent, gleaming deep within the shade of the tree. Everyone breathes gently, the birds are sated and Chalcy is relaxed, balanced, her aura clear, free from the shadowy smuts of anger, shame and fear. Grandma is kind and strong, wise and gentle, a safe haven for a child and like the wide shady branches of the oak tree, grandma's strength is derived from the deep roots of experience.

A lone black feather takes its final flight, a meandering descent, a lilting, undulating dance towards earth it alights upon Chalcy's right palm. With a dramatic flurry Chalcy jumps up, she points the feather forward, upward, and outward, spreading her arms like wings, her head bowed and shoulders stooped her legs step the ancient choreography intuited by the totem.

She sings "Tell it to the crows. Your stories and your woes. Tell it to the Crows." Again and again.

Chalcy's dancing figure highlighted by strands of sunlight jostling through the leafy canopy, golden shafts focus on outstretched arms creating ethereal wings of radiant light. The crows take flight, turning and twirling, cawing their strange melody.

Grandma watches in wonder. She asks "Has the world ever known such a child before?"

And the Crows respond. "She is only the beginning".

MAUREEN KRIVO

Like many of our contributing authors, Maureen Krivo's first taste of wriiting began in elementary school, when she wrote and illustrated a book about a big hairy creature who was afraid of vacuum cleaners.

She earned her Bachelor of Business Administration in Accounting from Kennesaw State University, then pursued "an assorted, motley mix" of jobs, but said being a writer is the only thing besides being a mom that ever meant anything to her.

Her genre preference is wide and varied, including Gothic, Fantasy, Paranormal and Young Adult fiction, but also Memoir, Narrative, and some poetry.

Maureen has written two novels. The first, <u>End of Penitence</u>, is "currently on a book shelf in the guest room, collecting dust." She is in the editing and re-writing stage of her second novel, <u>Blind Spot.</u>

Maureen is married to her best friend, Jeff, and they have one son, Jared. They also share their home with a "savage beast" named Lila.

A Round Tuit

"I hate you on opposite day." I could almost hear Michael's voice; see his mischievous smirk just inches from my face.

"Very mature, Michael," I murmured, remembering, as I stared down at his grave. Our conversations had never grown beyond witty gibes back and forth in school. It made sense that I had never visited his grave before. Why would I? I couldn't even say why I was there now. Wrapping my arms tighter around myself, I shivered against the late autumn chill.

"A friend of yours?"

I jumped back, startled by the elderly man in the worn gray trench coat standing behind me. His gnarled hands rested on a wooden cane, one on top of the other. He stared up at me intently, his bright eyes questioning and curious.

"Yes. Sort of. I guess," I replied, a little wary.

"It's been over twenty years," he observed, peering around me at the dates on the tombstone.

"Yes."

"When you picture him in your mind, is he smiling?" the man asked.

"I beg your pardon?"

The man said nothing, just kept smiling politely; waiting for me to answer. I decided he must be lonely, and that it wouldn't hurt to give him a few minutes of my time.

I shrugged. "I don't know. If I think about him long enough..."

"No. When you first picture him, is he smiling?" the man interrupted.

I blinked several times. "No," I finally stammered.

"Did he know how you felt about him?"

"I don't think so." I rubbed my hands together. "Why do you ask?"

Ignoring me, the man pressed on. "Why didn't you tell him?"

I looked around the cemetery then back to him. "I don't know. Never got around to it, I guess," I said.

The man held out a wooden coin with the words "A Round Tuit" carved into one side.

I chuckled. "Clever."

He nodded at the coin in his hand, encouraging me to take it.

Eager to be alone again, I took the coin. As the smooth wood touched my palm, the air rushed from my lungs and my vision blurred. Then, just as suddenly, I found myself sitting in Mr. Foster's drama class – just as I had twenty-one years before. I glanced around at my old friends and classmates. They looked so young!

I felt Michael's presence before I saw him. I looked up - the way you look up when you unexpectedly catch the scent of something wild and lovely, like honeysuckle or jasmine. Not that Michael was particularly lovely. He was moody and sarcastic, funny and deep. Different from anyone I had ever met.

He swept into the room just as the bell rang. Typical. Sliding into the seat next to mine, he leered over as though he was about to say something exasperating, but my vision blurred again.

The next instant, I was sitting on my bed in my old room, clutching a newspaper in my hands. "Senior Michael O'Conner...auto accident...miraculously survived...coma...brain damage...therapy."

Another blur.

I was standing by my old car in the near-deserted parking lot of the library. It was dark, except for a lone streetlight near the entrance. I made out the form of a person lurching and hobbling toward me. Michael. He called my name, his speech lagging and slurred.

But this time I didn't pretend not to hear him; I didn't shudder at his scarred and disfigured face when he got closer. This time I stood still – and even smiled – when he threw his arms around me. This time I hugged him back. I didn't shrink away in fear; didn't dive into the safety of my car; didn't ask him to leave me alone; didn't drive away with the image of his hurt and confused face imprinted on my heart.

Instead, I asked Michael if I could drive him home. He nodded enthusiastically. On the way, I told him how much I had missed him, his face beaming the whole time. When we got to his house, I helped him from the car. He turned to me with a lopsided grin. "I sill hape you on opp'sit day," he said slowly.

I laughed. "Real mature, Michael."

One last blur and I was standing alone in the cemetery again, the Round Tuit still in my hand. I looked at the tombstone, remembering.

Michael died of a brain aneurysm later that night, not long after I saw him in the library parking lot all those years ago. Nothing could change that. And yet somehow, through that ridiculous, little wooden Round Tuit – a gift from a stranger - I'd been given a chance to transcend time and space, just for a moment, and change *myself*.

I looked around for the old man. I wanted to thank him, but he was gone. I pictured Michael again. He was smiling this time. And so was I.

DEBRA MIHALIC STAPLES

Debra Mihalic Staples has built her career around the written word, as a freelance writer, editor and proofreader, but her interest in writing began in the 2nd grade when she had one of her short stories published in the local newspaper.

She earned her Bachelor's degree in Marketing from Florida State University, then studied English in the graduate program at the University of South Carolina.

A writer of both fiction and personal essays, Debra participated in her first FoxTale Book Shoppe Critique Workshop in October, where she received high praise for her work from her fellow participants.

A wife, and mother of twin daughters, Debra is currently working on writing a novel.

The Tumbleweeds

It had not been a great day so far, but it took a sharp turn for the worse when she found herself trapped in a Wyoming rest stop bathroom by a giant tumbleweed. Audrey exited the stall and stared at the monster ball of twigs now wedged in the doorway. It was nearly as tall as she was. The wind whistled through it with a desolate sound, just like the soundtrack of an old western. She shoved at it with her foot; some of the branches broke off, but it didn't budge. She had to struggle to yank her foot free. Tumbleweeds always seemed spindly when you saw them rolling along, but it turned out they were much tougher than they looked.

The relentless wind was to blame; it had slammed at the car as she drove, had propelled her toward the restroom, then had apparently crammed the tumbleweed into the open doorway in her wake. She shivered—it was a ridiculous thought, but it was like that thing had been following her. Squeezing between the wall and the partly open door, she pushed the door with all her strength, hoping to dislodge the tumbleweed, but it just pushed back against the door.

Shivering in her thin cotton T-shirt, she stood on tiptoe; she could see over the tumbleweed into the empty parking lot, with the empty highway stretching beyond it in both directions. She had seen only two vehicles during her three hours on the road. It could be a while before anyone came. There was no cellphone signal here; there hadn't been for miles.

Tears that had been just under the surface for months spilled over. There was no need to hide them now—Nathan wasn't there to see them. He grew irritated around displays of emotion, so she'd learned to hide her feelings. Therefore, when last winter she finally admitted she was unhappy in Wyoming, he was surprised.

"I didn't realize you were so homesick. Give it time, it will pass," he said. But she figured if it were going to "pass," it would have by then; they had been in Wyoming for five years.

Over brunch this past Labor Day she'd told him she was going back to Tennessee in a few weeks. He looked up and stopped chewing. Then he shook his head.

"You know I can't travel until the semester is over."

She stared at him. He thought she was just going for a visit and wanted him to come along. Suddenly she didn't want to have that discussion.

"Well, I want to see the leaves change, and I plan to drive, so I need to get going before the snow starts here."

He didn't know she had quit her job at the library and had been packing and shipping her books and clothes, box by box, to her sister's house in Johnson City. She hadn't made an effort to hide it, really—he just hadn't been around to see the evidence.

When she was leaving yesterday morning, Nathan had held her and kissed the top of her head.

"Call me when you get there," he said.

Then he turned away to wander through his xeriscape garden plots, bending now and then to pick at something.

She'd watched him in the rear view mirror until he was out of sight, but he never looked up. He didn't know she wasn't coming back. Or maybe he did. With Nathan you could never tell.

Now she wiped her eyes, then pulled some toilet tissue from the stall and blew her nose. Her mind raced along with her pulse; the restroom was spacious, but the fact that she couldn't get out was making her claustrophobic. She closed her eyes, tried to tune out the hum of the fluorescent lights, and focused on breathing in, breathing out, breathing in ... but the feeling that the tumbleweed was *watching* her made her open her eyes and glare at it. Its dry, seed-laden visage held a blank expression.

Maybe if she tried to close the door against it again, and kept shoving with it, she could dislodge the tumbleweed and send it on its way across the flats to pile up with its kin against a fence. But repeated tries only left her with a wrenched shoulder, and she caught herself wishing Nathan was there to rub it and soothe out the pain. That was something was good at that.

Those hands of his. They were smaller than you'd expect for a man of his size, yet when he took hold of a branch and asked his students whether the leaves in question were oblong or lanceolate in shape, you sensed their strength. He'd been her freshman year Botany 101 instructor when he was in graduate school. While her female classmates murmured about his outdoorsy good looks as he led them around the campus grounds identifying leaf types, she'd been captivated by his hands.

But they couldn't fix everything. They couldn't find the reset switch that would stop her from yearning for the green moisture of the eastern landscape and make her appreciate the arid beauty of the high desert. She'd tried. But when Nathan got tenure, it hit her like a rock to the head: He would not be moving back east, not for a long time, maybe not ever. The thought of not returning *home* shocked her with almost physical pain, and she suddenly realized she'd been living for the day when they could go back to Tennessee.

Their visits back home had only fueled her longing. She always tried to schedule their flight to arrive in the daylight so she could see the Appalachians on the approach, because that first glimpse of the waves of breathing green mountains lit her up inside. Even when she couldn't see the mountains because they were shrouded in banks of cloud, it still made her soul sing; all that moisture, just looking for a place to fall.

The second summer after they moved to Wyoming, they drove all day to visit Yellowstone. She'd fallen asleep while Nathan drove, and when she woke up surrounded by a vacant, sagebrush-spotted landscape, she had a brief panicked moment thinking they'd somehow survived an apocalypse and all of the trees were gone. When she told Nathan this, he chuckled and assured her that this land was deceptively active with life. He loved the high desert; its flora was his passion and his area of expertise.

The openness of the landscape, its great expanse, overwhelmed her. She had read accounts of pioneers on the prairie who had become so hopeless in the wind-lashed landscape that one day they'd just walked away from their lives toward the horizon, giving themselves up to the elements. She suspected that she might have more in common with those folks than she did with Nathan.

Her head snapped up as she heard a vehicle

approaching on the highway. Surely it would stop; rest areas and towns were far-flung in these parts. She stretched to look over the tumbleweed. A long tan RV sailed past the turn-in and kept going as she watched open-mouthed. According to her watch, she'd been here almost an hour, and that was the only vehicle that had appeared.

If she didn't get out of here soon, she wouldn't make it to Abilene before the candy factory store closed for the day. This damn tumbleweed was standing between her and a big box of assorted creme-filled chocolates. She was dreading that drive across Kansas, and the chocolate was something to look forward to.

Funny, when she'd first seen tumbleweeds, she was fascinated. There was something comical in the way they moved across the land, rolling until they bumped up against something, collecting against the side of a building or a fence like enormous dust bunnies.

Nathan explained how they weren't native plants, but Russian thistle that had been introduced, probably hitching rides with flax seeds brought to South Dakota in the late 1800s by Russian immigrants. They'd spread like crazy because they broke loose and rolled, scattering seeds as they traveled. Lots of animals ate them while they grew in the ground, and several bird species ate the seeds.

He'd heard about a town in Arizona that stacked them up to create the community's Christmas tree and a place in New Mexico where it was a winter tradition to construct a tall snowman out of tumbleweeds. Some woman was even selling them on the Internet. He'd been excited when he learned about research using Russian thistle to soak up depleted uranium from soils at nuclear weapons test sites.

Maybe this one had escaped from one of those sites. Maybe the radiation had mutated it into this sentient, mobile superweed. She was beginning to feel lightheaded.

Not only was she hungry, but all of her snacks were in the car. The only edible thing she found in her purse was a peppermint candy from the Mexican restaurant she and Nathan frequented. She popped it in her mouth.

Maybe it was the sugar rush that caused her to take a few running steps and hurl herself against the tumbleweed. It clutched at her as she howled. The seemingly delicate branches wore ragged barbs that pierced her skin. She pulled herself free, getting more lacerated in the process, and stared at the lacework of deep scratches down her arms and her legs below the hem of her capris. Red lines welled up and began to sting. She dampened a paper towel and blotted at the blood, clenching her teeth as the cold water met her irritated skin.

She bent over and rested her head on her folded arms against the damp edge of the sink, breathing in the faint chemical smell of disinfectant. Sooner or later, someone would come and help. Maintenance people, maybe, or a state trooper who passed by more than once and noticed that her car in the parking lot had not moved. Then came the unwelcome thought that, just as likely, someone less savory and more opportunistic might stop in this isolated place.

How had she allowed this to happen to herself? How far back would she have to go to find the moment when she'd set herself up for something like this?

She'd been born in Chattanooga, but had grown up moving from city to city along the east coast with her father's sales job, always poised for the next new neighborhood, the next new school. When she'd landed back in east Tennessee for college, it had been a relief; she could look forward to four years in one place! Then she fell in love with Nathan, and after she graduated, he asked her to move in with him and stay while he finished his doctorate. She did, mostly because she loved him, but also because she'd been content to remain in the mountain town.

Later, when he decided to take the job in Wyoming and asked her to come, she'd said yes. It had felt normal to let the man in her life decide where she lived.

For a while it had been an adventure. Not anymore. Nathan meant to spend the rest of his life here, with or without her. She didn't love him enough to spend the rest of her life feeling like she'd been broken off at the roots. She was no tumbleweed.

She straightened and took a slow, deep breath. The wind gusted, whining and whistling through the branches of the tumbleweed. Behind her, the stall door, sagging on one hinge, swung back and forth, bumping at the latch.

She had a flashback to a long-ago basic physics class. Within a few minutes, she'd wrestled the door off its remaining hinge and propped it on the side of a metal trash can she kicked over. Using this makeshift fulcrum and lever, she shoved at the bottom of the tumbleweed and then tried to force it free by pushing down on the upper end of the door. It didn't budge, but the door's edge gouged a depression in the weed's bulk— the beginning of a tunnel.

The stall door became a battering ram. She held it on its side and shoved, slid it back and shoved, kept pummeling at the tumbleweed until the door broke through to the other side. Sweating, her lacerations burning now, she knelt down and peered through the hole. She could see the front of her car.

She rammed and pulled the door back, shoved it and scooted it back again, until the muscles in her arms and shoulders cramped. Stopping to rest, she tried not to think of the germs on the floor grinding into the scratches on her legs as she knelt on the concrete to check her progress. She repositioned the door and rammed some more, all the time widening the hole. Each time when she squatted down to check its size, the wind blew grit into her eyes through it, but she blinked it away and kept going, a tunneling machine.

At last she stood up, certain the hole was big enough to crawl through. She wanted to plunge through it, but the trails of pain along her arms and legs reminded her of her earlier mistake. She checked the stalls and found two half-full rolls of toilet tissue, plus a spare full roll. It took some time to wrap each of her limbs, then her neck and head, leaving only her face uncovered.

Clutching her purse's strap in her teeth, she got down on her hands and knees and crawled into the twiggy tunnel, feeling broken ends of branches picking at her tissue shroud. It felt like the tumbleweed was trying to consume her. The tissue made whispery sounds as it tore and shredded; without it, that would be her skin.

When she crept out the other side and scrambled to her feet, the sidewalk was littered with bits of the tumbleweed's dry sticks and leaves, its progeny scattered all throughout the debris. She shuddered at the thought of how many new plants could be spawned from this mega weed as she peeled and yanked the tissue away in handfuls and stuffed it into the trashcan. She shook out her hair and brushed off her clothes and shoes. She didn't want to be an unwitting host, bearing the seeds to new fertile ground.

Wind gusts shoved at her as she hurried to the car, remembering the tub of trail mix in the front seat. She got in, yanked off the lid, and stuffed a fistful of peanuts, dried cranberries, and chocolate chips into her mouth, chewing hard as she fastened her seatbelt and started the car. She shifted into reverse, then turned to look over her shoulder.

All she could see was another tumbleweed, looming ever larger in her rear window as it rolled toward the car.

She bared her teeth and hit the gas.

BETSY SCOTT

It's been said that fiction is often based on real situations and people in a writer's life. That is true of the first story Betsy Scott wrote. It is about witches and she created the story from observing a strange lady in her neighborhood and the Atlanta child murders 1979-81.

Betsy earned her BA in Psychology, worked as a Paralegal for nine years, and was a licensed Realtor for three. But she has always enjoyed telling stories and decided to pursue a career in writing.

As a fiction writer, Betsy prefers penning mysteries with some humor, and hopes to publish a mystery series she is presently developing based on a young female realtor and her zany sidekick.

Married to George, with two adult children – Robert and Elizabeth, Betsy also shares her home with a golden retriever named Maggie.

Lost and Found

It was a bad idea from the start. Meg suspected the bodies were in this house, but finding them and getting proof out unscathed was another matter altogether. She had just begun to poke around, when her search was interrupted by the sound of someone's arrival through the back door. Meg scurried from the kitchen down to a partial basement to conceal herself. It was a miserable place, a combination of her trio of fears: darkness, spiders and small spaces. Moving slowly she crouched lower to avoid hitting the floor joists of the crawl space and cautiously moved deeper into the shadows managing in the process to run into a colossal spider web. The sticky threads covered her face, catching onto her eyelashes and lips. It took all she could muster to resist the urge to scream. Instead she managed to brush the web away by frantically waiving her hands across her face. Exhausted she flopped down behind one of the cinder block supports to listen and wait, hoping no one would discover she was there. At last, the sound of footsteps faded away and a door slammed. The rattling of the garage opening and the start of a car engine confirmed the departure of the resident. The house was hers once again.

"Damn", Meg whispered to herself. "That was close." This amateur sleuthing was fraught with risk particularly since she had neglected to anticipate problems as she concocted her strategy. She crept back up the stairs and pushed open the door. Across the room she noticed a second staircase leading to the upper floor. Without a moment's hesitation, she headed that way ignoring her inner voice warning her to get out of the house now.

Six months ago when she began her surveillance of this house she noticed the pattern of several large black sedans arriving and dropping off groups of unusual passengers dressed in long black robes, some carrying oversized bags. The women had been meeting here for months always at night. Initially Meg thought these meetings occurred randomly, but after comparing dates she recognized that the house meetings coincided with the recent missing children alerts in the city that year. There were now over 14 children missing.

Witches! Meg's wild imagination conjured up a coven as the reason for the strange gatherings of robed women. It wasn't much of a leap for her to tie in the missing children. Witches were known to like the flesh of innocent young children; Hansel and Gretel wasn't just a fairy tale it was based on tales of horrific practices that existed in the past and perhaps still prevailed today lurking on the edges of modern life. Meg couldn't imagine the pain the families of these missing innocent children endured. They had nothing to hold on to but fear and uncertainty. She was convinced she could prove her theory that the disappearances were related to the strange behaviors of these women and suspected she would find the dark truth buried somewhere within the bones of this house.

At the top of the stairs were three closed doors. The first room she entered had a large antique wardrobe against the far wall. The wardrobe was empty except for a few pieces of clothing piled on its bottom shelf. Behind it she could see the frame of a second door. It didn't take much for her to shove the bulky cupboard out of the way so she could access that second door. She placed her hand on the doorknob; heart pounding with trepidation, and twisted it to the right. Just as the door began to respond, she felt a blunt object smash into the back of her head followed by an all-consuming blackness as she lost consciousness.

The throbbing pain was relentless. She opened her eyes, tried to get up then realized her arms and legs were tied to the sides of the table she lay on. Almost immediately the smell in the room assaulted her. It was the heavy smell of an antiseptic solution. She squinted at the bright light that illuminated the room trying to see where she was. Then she heard the voice.

"Nosy people always find trouble." The voice of a woman came from behind her. "What to do with you; what to do?" The voice continued in a melodic tone.

Meg strained to twist her head around and see the owner

of that voice she heard. "Who are you, why am I tied up?" You need to release me right now. You have no right........." Then a hand squeezed her shoulder.

"Hush little girl, no need to worry now. Maybe you are the one who has no right, coming into my home uninvited and snooping around into things that are of no concern to you." Meg could tell from the clinking and stirring noises that the woman was working and mixing something at a counter just out of her field of vision. What she could see, as her eyes focused, was a room set up like a surgery. Stainless steel equipment, glass cabinets and hanging from the ceiling over the center of the room was a large industrial light. There were no windows.

Meg took a deep breath and continued her challenge. "So, are you hiding the children here? Where are they? What have you done with them?"

The woman chuckled, "You seem very sure of yourself. Would you really like to know the truth?" Her raspy voice continued. "Maybe we can reach an understanding. What exactly brought you here? Who are these children you speak of and why would you think I have these babies hidden in my home?

Meg moved her torso against the restraints trying to loosen them as she spoke. "Oh, I know a lot more than you realize. You are going to be sent away for a long time. My superiors know I am investigating you and they will be here very soon, since I haven't reported to them in the last two hours." This last little suggestion was not likely as Meg was just an inexperienced journalist with a vivid imagination. She was twenty three years old, a recent graduate, employed by the local newspaper for the past eighteen months to handle marriage and obituary notices. She had a lot to prove.

Her editor hadn't consented to this project. In fact no one knew she had planned this daring investigation involving breaking and entering. The only thing she had going for her was a passionate and determined attitude and that was not helping her at this point.

The door opened a second person came into the room and joined the woman at the counter. Their voices were low and muffled. Meg couldn't understand what was being said, but it sounded as if they were arguing. Then they approached her; two women who looked every bit like middle aged suburbanites fresh from their tennis match, no warts adorning large broken noises or long stringy black hair that were the accoutrements of story book witches. The taller of the two spoke first. "You are a smart young woman. It's a shame you have to end your journey here, but we can't risk it." The second one picked up Meg's right arm and swabbed it with a cotton ball soaked in alcohol.

Meg started thrashing about, but to no avail. She felt the sharp stab as a syringe penetrated the vein in her arm. The fogginess hit first, softening the hard edges and imbuing her with a cloudy dreaminess. The gurney was moving. They were taking her somewhere else in the house. She heard a door open and felt the rush of cold air over her body; it was dark except for the bits of daylight filtering through some small crevices. Someone released the ties on her arms and legs, but she could not move; whatever was in the injection had already paralyzed her limbs. She was lifted and placed gently on the floor. A hand brushed a strand of hair from her forehead, "Won't be long now dearie." She heard the door shut and a lock clink into place.

The quiet was eerily serene; she felt no pain. When her eyes adjusted to the dark she looked around in the dim room. Just on the edge of a shadowed corner across from where she lay, rows of stacked small boxes were visible. *Child sized coffins!* Her mind racing she began to count them. "One, two, three...." The drug's affect seized control of her tongue muscles, she could barely articulate. "Four, Fi, hix.............." she continued counting to the last box. "Foureen." Her lips strained to smile. *I found them!*

The End

Happily Ever After

    Clouds gathered overhead darkening the sky with an ominous message, nevertheless I continued down the path breathing in the damp salty air to the beach, the one place that gave me solace. Once closer to the shore, I lowered myself onto the warm sand and stretched out my legs pushing my feet thru the bits of broken shell and sand. The shallow surf barely reached me but the waves crept closer and closer with each approach teasing the edges of my hidden toes. At last I felt calm and sure of my decision. The cry of a gull interrupted my thoughts and I watched as the snow white creature landed in the edge of the surf; it seemed indifferent to me as it posed standing on one leg. I closed my eyes, and retraced the painful journey that brought me here.

***

    Two years ago in an impulsive moment I accepted Frank's proposal to marry. Just twenty-eight years old, I left my job, friends and home in the east with little thought given to the soundness of my decision. No analogy evaluated as to the suitability of this partnership other than my fear of being a designated an "old maid". It happened in a snap and before I could entertain second thoughts I was unpacking my suitcase in the small bedroom of an apartment in downtown Santa Monica, California.

    Our romance had struggled to life over a couple of years with typical disagreements and separations. Recently, Frank had taken a job as an analyst in Santa Monica. His move across the country was the catalyst that forced us to make a decision to continue our tumultuous relationship or end it. My youthful lust and naïve thinking that this marriage could work sealed my fate. It was a disaster from the beginning.

***

Frank was an Italian, seven years my senior, and could easily be the poster child for the hot blooded Mediterranean male. I was drawn to him the first time we met. He was my Adonis; a head of coal black tight curls, the sinewy body of a god and a face dominated by deep, sensuous brown eyes. But behind those eyes the beast was hidden. His passions in the bedroom enraptured me like the web of a spider as it ensnares its dinner, but this same hot current fueled a volcanic temper as well. Seemingly small matters would explode out of proportion. I vividly remember a morning we had planned a drive up the coastal highway to tour a local winery. As I prepared for the day my reflection in the mirror smiled back at me, a petite oval face with large azure blue eyes and a small nose sprinkled with a mob of freckles. Unlike most of my girlfriends, I was born with near perfect skin and never wore much makeup. Satisfied with a light application of lip gloss I struggled to place the lose pieces of my wispy sun streaked hair back into a pony tail then I slipped into a soft, cotton t-shirt tucking it into my jeans as I headed out of the bedroom. Grabbing my Nikes from the closet, I ran into the kitchen excited to spend the day with Frank on a romantic road tour. The moment I saw his expression, my fantasy vanished. "Are you really planning to go with me dressed like that? You look like some trailer trash from south Georgia!" He slammed his coffee mug down on the kitchen counter splattering the liquid across the laminate. Those brown eyes stared coldly at me then he turned and left the room. Tears silently fell as once again Frank's temper defined the day. This was the shadow in our marriage that randomly crept out and in a flash reduced a happy moment to disaster.

I was not prepared to face it in the daily doses delivered during our marriage. It was exhausting living with this volatile personality; I saw no choice but to try. So I struggled to anticipate his desires and avoid any manner of confrontation, a role more suited to a concubine than a beloved wife.

***

The darkness in Frank's personality rarely revealed itself during our courtship. It was camouflaged by his amorous and attentive maneuvers as he pursued me. "Short stuff" was the affectionate name he called me. Even though at five foot three I was average height for a woman. There were often gifts and outlandish surprises when Frank arrived, "Here is the tiniest token of my infinite love for you, Short Stuff." Laughing as he bowed before me and presented a single daisy." Obviously he had snatched it from my neighbor's garden, but it delighted me nonetheless. Even when Frank traveled, notes executed on his own personalized embossed stationery would appear in my mailbox filled with romantic script to let me know I was never far from his mind and heart. His attention and devotion was applied like a frosting to a cake,   smoothly and ever so thick; I was consumed by its sweetness.

***

Life in Santa Monica was difficult to adjust to and nothing like home. The unsettled environment surrounding our apartment fed my uneasiness. There were nights we would awaken to hear gunfire and bullet volleys across our apartment roof, not an uncommon occurrence in downtown prior to its gentrification. Frank would not tolerate my fear and anxiety. He spent his youth and a significant part of his adulthood in New York and Boston. The violent accoutrements of big city life were not frightening to him. "Get over yourself, it's part of life in a *real city*. You're so naive." That was all he offered to soothe my fear.

My lack of employment became another point of contention for Frank. A strong work ethic was dominant in Frank's personality and a valued attribute until it mutated when he applied it to me. When we first moved in together, he worked long hours and I was unemployed so he expected me to bear the housekeeping responsibilities cleaning, doing the laundry, shopping and cooking all our meals. It was critical to maintain our household to Frank's standards, the slightest deviation, could send him into a rage. Consumed with housekeeping perfection, I was left with little time to focus on a job search. Ironically, we didn't need the income, but nonetheless Frank was relentless in his harassment of me to find employment. The only path to peace was to do as he demanded.

It was not difficult. My background as a paralegal qualified me for several opportunities.   I submitted a few applications and received a call back for an interview at, Smith and Bards, LLP, a personal injury practice. Working for the injured and underdog suited me perfectly. When the job was offered my self-respect briefly flickered to life and those hopeless feelings faded like a bad dream.

With my additional income we were able to buy a small place north of the city. It was a bungalow about four blocks from the ocean and much quieter than in town. The close access to a beach was a blessing; it offered an easy escape and sweet relief for me. I tried to make a habit of walking there at every opportunity. As the weeks passed a routine, but false sense of calmness took over in our relationship. I began to believe that things had changed and our life together was improving.

"Let's take a walk on the beach after dinner. I'll help wash up the dishes." Frank suggested and smiled at me. We silently worked together; he washed, I dried. The sun was inching below the horizon casting an amber glow to the beach as we strolled along the beach in our bare feet. Frank reached for my hand. "Coming up on our first wedding anniversary aren't we, Short Stuff? Maybe we should plan a trip somewhere special." I didn't answer. My mind set the stage.

We're sitting at a beautiful table with elaborate spray of white roses and lilies as the center piece and set to the side, a bottle of champagne its moist condensation playfully running into the stark white napkin wrapped around its neck. Frank reaches across the table and affectionately traces his fingers down my slender arm.

It was a dangerous illusion.

***

One evening I had been delayed at work and Frank arrived home almost an hour before I did. Tardiness had often been a trigger for Frank's temper. Walking through the front door I was filled with trepidation. My face met the brunt force of the palm of Frank's hand as he slapped me squarely across my right cheek. "You bitch, where the hell have you been. Were you even planning to serve me dinner? I walk in and there's nothing here?" I was stunned as I bent over from the shock of his attack and wrapped my arms around my chest to protect myself. He grabbed me and pushed me into the kitchen continuing to rant about my failure as a wife and the fictional dinner he expected. He had never laid a hand on me before; it was always his loud angry voice and constant admonishments which over time had caused me to lose the girl I used to be. I was like a robot going through the motions of living with no joy, no anticipation; just sheer numbness all in the name of preserving our marriage.

An overriding sense of helplessness engulfed me that evening as I carefully placed a cold cloth on my raw cheek and swollen lips. I had locked myself in the bathroom. I couldn't imagine telling anyone what had happen. There was no one I would call. The utter horror that my husband had attacked me was both embarrassing and humiliating, but even worse the violence that came seemingly out of nowhere shattered the last fragment of self-respect I still possessed. Feelings of isolation and emptiness had grown like a tumor in my gut. This loneliness compounded by the vast distance created when I'd made the move away from family and friends. Home felt continents away. Staring at the black and white tile pattern on the floor, I mourned the loss of passed friendships and wondered how I could have made such a fatal mistake marrying Frank. There was no rewind button, no delete tab and no re-write.

***

Rain drops began hitting my face running down my cheeks like tears, but I had no feelings. The storm had intensified now accompanied by the distant rumble of thunder. As the surf slowly pulled back from the shore, I lifted myself and walked to the water's edge. Hesitating, I felt a tightening in my stomach. This was not the gentle solution I hoped it would be, but my mind offered up no imaginings of an alternative. The sharp coldness of the surf curled around my ankles and I moved forward. It crept up my calves. For a moment I lingered in the breakers staring at the horizon in anticipation of a release from my pain. The cry of the gull was the last sound I heard as I lowered myself and surrendered my body into the dark embrace of the water.

The End

VICTORIA LYNNE YODER

Victoria Lynne Yoder has spent her career inspiring students in the classroom, as an elementary school teacher working with remedial and gifted students. But her first foray into writing was "Ella's Vocabulary Book," which she wrote for her granddaughter.

She earned her BS of Education, and her Master's Degree with a focus on Gifted Education, then began her career in Warren, Michigan, where she taught for seven years. After moving to Georgia, Vikki spent 25 years teaching in Cobb County schools, including a Target Center in South Cobb County where she taught gifted students who were bussed in from 11 area schools.

Vikki's writing preferences include fiction, memoir and poetry, but she looks forward to sharing "Ella's Vocabulary Book" with a wide audience, as it introduces fun, rarely used words such as "fishmonger" and "gallimaufry" (which we have used in Creative Writing Class!).

Vikki is the proud mother of two grown daughters, Rebecca Diane Hough and Erin Elizabeth Davis; and grandmother to Ella Lynn and Olivia Claire, whose vocabularies promise to be impeccable!

A Place to Call My Own
Dedicated To: Burr Holloway, the builder of DREAMS

    It was an obscure awakening that stirred my ingenious idea to rummage through the attic. It was a dreary day, and I felt compelled to go on this attic adventure. There was something calling me, pulling me. I climbed the rickety steps to the attic and knew immediately what I was searching for this windy, chilling day in October.
    I began to relax, and I magnified in my mind the knotty pine circular table that my father had built for me many years ago. It was there, leaning sadly and forlorn against an old battered trunk. It was in two pieces with an A&P bag attached filled with the appropriate screws and nails. With the help of my dear friend, we positioned ourselves on the ladder and gingerly lowered the pedestal and the table top down the attic steps. We put it back together with the same precision in which it had been built so many years ago.
    I placed it in the Art Room, feeling heavy hearted, despondent, and a bit inconsolable. Why had I been so neglectful and negligent all these years, leaving the table alone in the dark dismal attic without giving it life?
    I entered into a mood, reminiscent of the glee I had while watching my father prepare the knotty pine wood with loving care. I began to recollect the creativity in my father's hands,

his steadfastness, and his devotion to perfection.

Suddenly, I began shifting desires in this room filled with pungent paint smells, bright colors, finished and unfinished works of art. Now it was beginning to come clear. The connotation that this was "just" my Art Room became extinct. This was my Room of Creativity. I had found my writing place.

DAWN T. WALKER

Dawn T. Walker earned her Bachelor of Arts in Journalism from the University of South Carolina before pursuing her career as a working artist, painter and sculptor, but a play she wrote for her acting class in high school provided a spotlight for her gift for the written word.

"I wrote a play... and my teacher asked me if I had copied it from somewhere. I said 'No,'" and decided that was a good compliment; she validated my work in a wacky kind of way."

Dawn is also a world traveler, and is currently working on a memoir of her trekking experiences and her work with non-profits.

She is the mother of three wonderful children.

Wild Ass, Initiation and Chili Peppers

    It was a burnt umber night soft glow around a full moon, throwing a sideways beam on the tall rock walls. In the daytime they turned a fiery alizarin red with a crisp twist of blue edging out of the cracks and screaming to be noticed. The roots of those hard rock mountains were extended deeply into the salt crust of a familiar earth.
    Moon lay her beam down helplessly searching for a perfect canvas. She had a thought. A random thought. Not one that sits and mulls about perfectly formulated but one that flashes like lightening. Her thought lingered as her eye blue beam settled upon a stallion. A beautiful being that seemed to be perfectly peeled from the infinite. He stood hoofing the pebbled space around him. Moon thought, "HMMMM are those red chili peppers hanging from the horses mane?" She threw the thought into a still corner near the horse.
    Wondrously the horse known by its owner as "Wild Ass" stepped back threw his head upward and winked. Now I've never seen a horse wink but Wild Ass could. Delighted Moon shot him another thought "Do you use those peppers to burn the longing out of the virgins who ride you?" Wild Ass reared up and shook his head back and forth "Is that a yes or no?" Moon asked.
    In the colorless night the last fringy edges of umber slipping softly away, Wild Ass or shortened version "Wild" just

took off running in that black poised way he always did without pause of thought.

Moon was baffled, not an unusual thing. She now thought her telepathic powers had as they say "left the room". She followed Wild with a steady focused beam. Chili peppers askew and bobbing to the cantering horse all she felt was curiosity and a sweet optimism. It was a kind of radical exuberance. I mean really, what else has a moon to do but just beam at all things static and those that blur into movement. "This is fun" she thought "even adventurous" which was the epitome of Wild, thus the name. The owner chose well.

Wild ran and ran into an abstract space. Abstract because he had no idea where he was going. Darkness lends itself to that skinny slim edge of being. Wild loved the dark at times. He loved to dance on the border of the metaphysical. It delighted him. He had learned how to live in that slender sorrow of "not knowing" and it had taught him that sorrow was not a necessity but a choice. If you flip it around, sorrow ceased and became a torch for the lightness of being that created a pathway to freedom. He knew that freedom. That is why he could hear the heart song of others.

Moon watched that fierce eager energy and she could not help but jump with glee. If she had hands they would have clapped, not a one handed ZEN clap, but a real clap. She thought "Where is he going to find Virgins in this stolen land?" Stolen from the Rock Goddesses, Mountain Gurus, and high circling falcons. Wild galloped and galloped over shards of solidified sand, fossilized shells, edgy edges and simple straight paths. Moon of course followed, having a fine old time.

"Where are the virgins?" she asked. Unanswered on and on Wild went until he didn't. Chest heaving, Wild stopped abruptly with a resolute stance. There standing in the numinous desert space she was. Waiting for Wild. A gaze solid soft but strong with a glow of compassion. She just held her arms open and waited. Moon was mesmerized. Wild hesitant, knew he had found his Virgin. Her heart song had been calling him all night long relentlessly with a deep sonorous thrum, as close as his own heartbeat. Moon threw another thought out this time to the Virgin "Why do you so persistently call?" The Virgin felt annoyed to hear such a silly question when the answer was clearly twinkling out from her gaze.

She looked up in that night sky which nested Moon and promptly flipped her the bird. A seamless movement really that needed no long thoughts, for the bones in her body were shaking awake. They uttered an ancient intuitive language, one that the Dakinis, "Sky Goers" had been whispering into her heart for years. She now had ears to hear a song that had always been buried within.

The silence that was, could no longer be or fall into the hidden crevasses that lay behind every hard rock place in her mind seizing joy.

So it was with a playful delight and a primal anger that she made that gesture. On the surface it seems like a rather radical gesture to send to Moon since she only threw down loving light but the Virgin had grown weary of a silence that wasn't really "noble" and she was irritable. On this night she unrobed that silence for good.

Moon caught the gesture with her eyes excited and wide. She had no comprehension of what it felt to not be softly whole. The horse took an awkward step forward and waited. The Virgin with a fierce leap jumped on Wilds back, tossed her veil to the ground (all Virgins wear veils) and threw her head back letting out a laughter that caught the edge of cackling. She yelled a sharp "Go!" using an authority she never knew was within. Her bones were talking now. The marrow of her soul could be silenced no longer.

She pulled off those tangled red chili peppers from Wild's mane. She no longer needed the shamanic healing burn they held to quiet the longing. She rode that horse like the wind and the wind lifted her over the desert and into any place she desired.

Liberation has a pure and sweet taste, one that doesn't get lost on a hungry tongue quickly. I don't know how a moon bows, but that night she did.

ROGER BROOKS WILSON, SR.
aka Roger "Hurricane" Wilson

Roger Wilson penned his first story about a superhero, when he was in grammar school, but his first published piece was a letter to the editor of Boy's Life (the Boy Scouts of America magazine), when he was 12.

After graduating from Woodward Academy in College Park, GA, Roger attended Brookdale Community College in Lincroft, NJ, and earned his Associate of Arts degree in Business from Floyd College in Rome, GA.

Throughout his formative years, Roger pursued music in all its forms. His 43-year music and broadcasting career includes guitar instructor, touring musician, songwriter, record company owner, music publishing company owner, broadcast producer, and journalist.

He has toured more than a million miles, recorded more than 16 CDs, and was inducted into the Oklahoma Blues Hall of Fame in 2015 for his involvement in music education. The stories here are just a small part of his journey.

Roger is married to Julia Gaydosh Wilson, and is the father of two grown sons – Roger Wilson, Jr., and Ryan Wilson, with his first wife, Ginger. He is currently working on writing and editing his memoir.

The Amazing Les Paul

We were all saddened by the loss of the legendary guitarist and inventor, Les Paul. He completely changed the world of music with his creation of sound-on-sound recording, as well as the invention of the solid body electric guitar. Many know that he crossed numerous boundaries by winning multiple awards for his achievements, as well as inductions to various halls of fame. Many obituaries, tributes, and eulogies are still being written about Les Paul. When I was in the broadcast news business, one of my bosses told me, "If you are going to write something, tell me something I don't know!" Well here goes! It is true that for me, being friends with a guy like Les Paul would never be an unwanted attribute, but in my case, it was truly unexpected.

In September of 2003, I was on tour in the Northeast, and I decided to catch one of Les Paul's weekly shows in New York City. A couple of friends and I decided to make the trip to the Iridium Jazz Club near Times Square for Les's weekly Monday night show. After paying the thirty or so dollars each to get in, we were there! I was really excited to be able to see this man in action, one of my idols, a man that I had read about for so many years. Plus, all those years playing the model of guitar named after him... The Gibson Les Paul! I had determined that I was going to make this night pleasurable and go easy on myself. I wasn't going to try to get an autograph, or get on stage, schmooze, hustle, or do any kind of PR or music business. It was just going to be a guitar lesson for me.

The lights went down, and Tom, the sound man announced, "And now the man that has changed the course of popular *music for all of us, Mr. Les Paul and his trio."* It was amazing, and I was enthralled! There he was, in the flesh... the guy that invented multi-track recording, and the solid body electric guitar. I was savoring the moment and I was oblivious to everything else around me. This was what I had been waiting for. After about 3 or 4 songs, Les starting cutting up with the crowd and the band. He was really quick and really funny. This talent, no doubt, had to have carried over from his early days in vaudeville.

It seemed that someone on the front row was talking to him. Whoever it was had said something on the order of "I play guitar too". Les replied, "So you play too, eh? Well come on up here and show us what you can do." At that moment, a well-dressed gentleman from India approached the stage. He strapped on the guitar that Les keeps on the piano for just such occasions. I wasn't sure what was happening here, but I was trying to figure it out. The guy started playing the introduction to T-Bone Walker's Stormy Monday... BADLY! Now I was getting worried! The hair on the back of my neck was starting to stand up. My friends, Bobby and John, knew I was starting to get restless. I was trying to keep from turning green and to not have my clothes split off me like The Incredible Hulk. The guy played the one song, and he was off the stage. It really wasn't a pretty site. By this time, I was fit to be tied, mainly because I couldn't leave this night with that vision in my head. Was it a joke? Was it planned? There was no way to tell. Not sure of what would happen next, Les resumed his show as if nothing had happened. I did eventually calm down to enjoy the rest of the set. It was a truly wonderful experience, once the whatever it was interruption had passed.

At the close of this, the first show, the announcement was made that CD's could be purchased from Les's son, Rusty. I immediately went to him, bought a CD, and asked him if that last appearance had been planned. He said that they had never seen the guy before. Again, somehow, there was no way I was going to leave here this night with that vision of that first guy with a guitar in my head. I explained to Rusty who I was, that I was on tour, and that I had my first Les Paul guitar when I was 18. He said if he had known I was there, they would have gotten me up there. "Well," I said, "I am still here." He said OK, come on back and I'll introduce you to Dad. I was caught off guard by his response and ecstatic at the same time!

When I met Les, it was like talking to an old friend. I explained to him my situation just coming to listen and to pay my respects. In asking me if I would like to sit in, I told him that wasn't my reason for attending his show, but after the train wreck I witnessed earlier in the set, I simply said, "Yes, I would like that very much." He seemed pleased and said for me to stand by the stage and that he would get me up with him. I did that and was trying to control my excitement. In the next set, he called me up with no idea of who I was or what I could do. I introduced myself to the audience over the microphone telling them my name and how honored I was to be there. I immediately launched into a simple version of "Everyday I Have the Blues", with the band following. As I played and sang, Les was smiling. After that song, he said, "Well what else ya got?" I went into a slow B.B. King Blues classic, "Sweet Little Angel". That was surreal since, I made it to the second song!" Les and I swapped some licks back and forth. He and I were having a ball! The first guy got the hook after the first tune. I made it to the second song. When I came off stage, I was walking on air.... is was a day I would never forget!

  Over the next few years, I would return to jam with Les and the band about half dozen times. I became friends with the band and crew, Lou, Nicki, John, Tom, and Chris. Les's son, Rusty and I would stay in touch. During my trips to the northeast, I would attend his Sunday night jams at various locations around northern New Jersey, and then go into the city to see Les on Monday. The stories I was hearing from him were priceless. He told me how he got Mary Ford to speak into a microphone down the hall, and when he heard her voice repeated on the extra tape head he installed, he knew he had found the thing that would change music recording forever. He told Mary to grab the laundry, throw it in the car, and that they were heading to Chicago. She kept saying, "What if it doesn't work?" During that trip from California, by the time they were in New Mexico, he was wondering if it would work. He then said, "By the time we got to Chicago, I had convinced myself that it wasn't going to work". He was thankful that when they drilled the first hole in a new Ampex tape recorder in Chicago to add the extra record head, that "we didn't screw anything up!" That would be the beginning of sound on sound recording technology.

  During another of my visits, Les simply said, "Man, if I was to ever retire, I would just die!" He was 89 then! Another time, I was helping the guys carry some gear up to the street to put in the car. After 2 shows, he had signed autographs for a line of people that circled the inside of the club. He had signed everything from guitars to pictures, to records, to pick guards, to you name it! After signing every last item, Les was still downstairs in the rest room. As I headed back in, the manager at the door with keys to lock up said, "What did you forget?" I said Les is still in the club! I ran back down and got him. I'll never forget Les Paul holding on to my arm as we climbed the stairs at 1 A.M.

When he turned 90, it seemed that the world showed up to witness him. The crowds were lined up out the door at the Iridium on Monday nights. Interviewers from all walks of media were at the dressing room door for weeks before and after his birthday. I had the pleasure of sitting in with him 3 days before his actual 90th. The big event was a couple of weeks later at a star-studded event in Carnegie Hall.

My last visit with him was in November of 2007, at age 92. When my friend, Bobby Lyons, and I arrived at the Iridium early, Les was having his usual dinner in the dressing room. He was always eating his dinner off of an audio monitor cabinet, turned on its side. I always wondered why they didn't get him a small table in there. It seems that a little better treatment would be in order. This time, when I arrived, Les responded and waved slowly. It was a little disconcerting to me. We then decided to grab a bite before the show. When I returned, I happened to be in a position to help him on to the stage. He seemed to appreciate it by patting me on the back as he went up the few stage steps. He ambled to his chair, picked up his guitar, and as soon as the introduction announcement was made and the lights came up, "It Was Showtime!" He was back! I got to sit in both sets that night! After the second show, he came back into the dressing room, collapsed on the couch and said, "Man I'm Tired!" I said, "Les! Are you OK? I was really quite concerned about you earlier." He said, "Oh yea, I'm fine. I've just been putting in these 14 hour days". I replied, "14 hour days! What are you doing?" He said, "I'm still working on these guitars". "What are you doing to them?" I asked. "I'm still trying to get that sound right!" I was amazed! This is why he would jump out of bed every morning until the end ...to keep "chasing sound."

There is no doubt that Les Paul, as an inventor, actually picked up where Thomas Edison left off regarding the development of sound technology. Of course we have to realize that there will be future generations that will pick up where Les left off. This was evident when Apple Computers Co-Founder Steve Wozniak showed up one Monday night to Les's dressing room at the Iridium while I was there. While Les notably continued Edison's developments, Steve Wozniak and

Steve Jobs picked up the ball and ran with it in taking music and audio technology to an all new level. There were some interesting conversations that evening between Steve Wozniak and Les Paul that I won't even begin to describe. It was just satisfying to know I was there first hand to witness it.

The amazing thing about Les is that with as many important and well-known people that he associated and rubbed shoulders with, he would always show his fondness for guys like me who just loved to play guitar. He would sign guitars when I would take them in to his show. He would always write something nice on them. "Keep on picking" was a favorite, but the night he wrote, "Those Were Some Great Blues!" I was pretty well knocked out.

Les actually confessed to me that since he was more commercially oriented, he didn't know much about the history of the Blues. He asked me to explain it to him. I sat in the dressing room of the Iridium one night and gave him my basic simple interpretation of the origin of the Blues. He sat there listening carefully, really soaking it in. I couldn't believe that Les Paul was actually learning something from me! During the month of June, 2009, I attended one of Rusty Paul's jams in New Jersey. My plan was to go into New York City on the Monday afterward to see Les. Rusty told me that Les hadn't been able to make some shows in the last few weeks and he had been in and out of the hospital. He had even missed his 94th birthday gig on June 9. I was concerned about it, but Rusty said his Dad was doing better, and was itching to get back to work. If I knew anything at all about Les, I knew that was true. He said that his Monday gigs at the Iridium were just like celebrating New Year's Eve every week. About a month and a half later, I flew back home to Atlanta for a few days off from the road. As I was driving to pick up a new shipment of CD's, I received a call from my friend Bobby in New York telling me that Les had just passed. Though not unexpected, it was still a very sad day.

Since that time, I have been in touch with his son, Rusty Paul, on a regular basis, as well as band members, jazz guitarist Lou Pallo, pianist John Colliani, and upright bassist Nicki Parrot, from time to time on social media. Les's grandson, Stephen Paul, owns and operates a restaurant called The Rusty Moose in Alton, New Hampshire. It has been a pleasure for me to become good friends with Stephen, and to perform at his establishment from time to time.

Les Paul proved to me many times that having a passion for something in life will keep one alive. For a guy like Les

Paul, and with a life like he had, we can't afford to mourn his loss as much as we need to always remember and celebrate his life. We all need to *"KEEP ON PICKING", and to keep "CHASING THAT SOUND!!!"*

My Friend, Andy Rooney

Andy Rooney was known by everyone. He was a household name. You either loved him or hated him. Many folks agreed with him and many disagreed with him. Andy was most familiar to America as the curmudgeonly and grouchy commentator closing out CBS weekly 60 Minutes news documentary since the 70's. Having listened to his commentaries for many years, I was always intrigued by the way he could write just about anything and everything. During an interview on CNN with Larry King, he actually said that he could write about the head of a pin. In completing one of his books, he was right. He wrote about things he liked and things he didn't, along with things he would and wouldn't do. During one commentary, he had an array of sport drinks on his desk. Being inquisitive of what some of the drinks tasted like by looking at the color, he said that he would never drink anything "blue".

Somehow a paperback book written by Andy had found me. After reading it, I handed it off to someone else. While shopping at a second hand store on the road somewhere in Indiana, a couple of hard copies of Andy's caught my eye. Of course I bought them. Upon completing the first one, Andy seemed like a long lost friend, and I almost felt like I knew him. There were certain conditions that he put across to his readers. He wouldn't just sign anything, but he would sign his books or his photos if asked. He also mentioned that he enjoyed being complimented for his work. Who doesn't! Knowing some of his conditions, I slipped a note into the book and mailed it to him in New York requesting an autograph. I really attempted to stay within his required parameters. A self-addressed postage paid envelope was also included. Sometime later, the book showed up in the mail at my home.... Signed, Andrew Rooney! It made me very happy.

A year or two later, I was sitting in my motorhome on the Wyoming prairie outside of a club I was working in when I completed a second book of Andy's. Instead of having the book bounce around the RV while traveling, writing a quick note to Andy and putting it in the mail to him seemed like a better idea. I decided to include a note to Andy letting him know that I would be in New York City in a few weeks visiting and sitting in with Les Paul and his trio at the Iridium Jazz Club at his regular Monday night show. The note was handwritten on a yellow legal pad since I didn't have a printer in the motorhome. The book and note were mailed and forgotten about. While I was in Arizona a few weeks later, my wife told me that I received a personal letter from Andy Rooney, along with the second autographed book. He had typed a note to me on his Royal typewriter, actually crossing out a wrong letter with a pencil. Saying he enjoyed receiving the letter, he admitted that he actually remembered what the letters of the alphabet looked like. It appeared that Andy was impressed that I had actually taken the time to hold a pen and actually expend the energy to write to him manually as opposed to typing on a computer. He mentioned that he knew nothing about music and couldn't tell one instrument from the other when listening. He did mention a musician friend of his that had passed away within the last few years. That was the extent of any musical conversation. Andy also included his phone number and invited me to visit him at CBS when I arrived in New York.

In the fall a few months later, I called Andy to tell him I was in the area. We agreed that I would visit with him on a Tuesday, after sitting in at Les Paul's show the Monday night before. On the way into New York City from the suburbs on Monday night, with my friend Bobby Lyons driving as he always did, I left a voice mail for Andy, inviting him to come into the Iridium while I was there. I didn't think he would show up, but I didn't want to rule it out, should he choose to accept the invitation.

There was only a twelve hour turnaround before I was back on the bus Tuesday morning from Pearl River, NY to keep my appointment with Andy. When contacting him on my phone, he asked where I was. He laughed when I told him I was on the bus. After arriving at the CBS Network and being admitted through security with a guest pass, I rode the elevator to Andy's office. When I walked in, there he was, the man, Andy Rooney! He was avidly typing away. He immediately stopped and shook my hand, saying that I was much taller than he pictured. I told him he was exactly as I pictured. In showing him a photo in my camera from the night before with Les Paul, he said that he almost showed up at the Iridium. He said, "When I left work, I drove around the block and I saw the people standing outside the club. I knew you were in there, but I just went on home."

We sat and talked for a little while about various things, mostly things I knew about him from his book. There were so many things going through my mind, but we just proceeded to have a very cordial visit. He also introduced me to Keith, his producer, and to Susie, his assistant. They were folks I knew about through his books and occasionally from his weekly 60 Minutes features. Having read several of his books by this time, I think I knew Andy pretty well, as well as a little about his wife and children that he mentioned periodically.

Andy also enjoyed woodworking at his home in Connecticut and at his vacation home in Upstate New York. He had spoken about that in his books. The desk that he sat behind for many years for his weekly 60 Minutes features was a piece of furniture that Andy cut from a huge tree himself. I marveled at that for a few minutes. He showed me around his office and studio, telling me of some future pieces he was working on.

Here I was in Andy's little world that he loved. CBS had given him free reign to do what he loved doing best... to write. He was in a separate area of the building more or less detached from the rest of the CBS operation. His history was amazing. His first job was in the military writing for the publication Stars & Stripes. Andy flew with many bombing missions over Normandy, writing the stories as they happened. The pilots were each to fly twenty-five bombing missions, and their jobs would be done. That is if they survived. He spoke emotionally about going to breakfast with many of the guys some mornings, and of the empty places at the table in the evenings of the ones that didn't return. His book, My War, tells the full story of his years in the U.S. Army. Andy's broadcast career also spanned many decades, having written for Harry Reasoner and Arthur Godfrey along the way. No matter what Andy wrote about, I loved reading about it. Toward the end of the visit, Andy agreed to let me sit behind his desk with him for a picture. He also signed another couple of books for me. That was a great day.

I made another visit to Andy a year later on a return visit to New York. This time, I made it a point to bring his book, My War, for him to sign. He began telling me of an event he attended the night before that had Tom Brokaw as the featured speaker. Andy loved Brokaw. He said, "Tom is just so smart and so articulate... he is just the best there is." At the same time I replied, "Well Andy, I believe that Tom Brokaw wrote the forward in your book, My War, that I brought for you to sign." He said, "Really?" I said, "Yes, I believe so", having recalled seeing Brokaw's name in the book. "Here it is," as I passed the book to Andy. He thumbed through the front of the book and actually didn't realize that Tom Brokaw had written the forward in his book. I believe that he just probably forgot about it. Upon appearing to remember while seeing it in black and white, he seemed very impressed. At the end of this visit, Andy invited me to come back and see him next year, "If I'm still here," he said. He also gave me a couple of his latest books, signed of course.

Back on the bus, I began reading one of the latest books he gave me. Right in the front, Andy wrote that the book was dedicated to his wife, who had passed away four years earlier. I felt bad that I didn't know, but I immediately understood why he had said he had a small apartment in the city as opposed to commuting back and forth to Connecticut each day. This was my last visit, but we still stayed in touch.

      Sometime later, I kept reflecting on my visits with Andy, and how fortunate I was to have spent the time with him that I did. He wasn't the kind of guy to interact with viewers very often, if at all. It seems that I approached him the right way at just the right time. Suddenly I felt that I needed to write a song about Andy. When I finished THE BALLAD OF ANDY ROONEY, I sent him an advance copy. Whether or not he liked it, I'm not sure. If I were to guess, he probably thought himself not worthy of such a tribute. The final version was recorded in Nashville and was released as a single, as well as appearing on my 2010 CD, THE RAINBOW UP AHEAD on Bluestorm Records. I made sure that Andy, along with his colleagues at 60 Minutes, received copies. I'm told they got a kick out of the song. Andy passed away on November 4, 2011 after complications from a minor surgery procedure. The utmost tribute that could have been paid to Andy Rooney was for CBS not to replace him with anybody to fill the empty spot at the end of 60 Minutes. I commend them for that.

Hee Haw Revisited

For those that have never heard of the TV show Hee Haw, it was a cornball comedy satirizing rural life. The hosts were legendary guitarist Roy Clark and country music icon Buck Owens. Some of the characters that appeared regularly and from time to time were well known Grand Ol' Opry stars such as Grandpa Jones, Minnie Pearl, Little Jimmy Dickens, and Stringbean. The show was popular throughout the seventies. My grandma was a big fan of Hee Haw. The show was hard to take seriously, but it had its moments. All Hee Haw was to me for a while was what my band and I referred to as a road alarm clock. When we were on the road in the late seventies and early eighties, when Hee Haw came on TV in the hotel room, that was our cue to get ready to go to the gig.

My other memory is one of my grandma talking about a newscast describing the murder of a Hee Haw cast member in the early seventies. In overhearing her describe the story to my mom at the time, she was sadden by the death of Stringbean, one of the show's primary characters. Stringbean was a wiry fun loving and banjo playing funny man that had developed a loyal following among viewers. He had been murdered, although the details had never been made clear to me. Nothing much was ever heard about the story again until years later.

A friend of mine in Nashville, Jim Boyd, was someone I met through sobriety channels. He is a successful Music City commercial real estate developer with a big heart. He had been conducting AA meetings in the maximum security prisons in Nashville for a number of years. While in Nashville, I accompanied him to a couple of meetings in a couple of the high security facilities. The first one we attended together was at the special needs prison. It was a regular weekly meeting with each person telling their story. One gentleman named John seemed to be the guy in charge from the way he was answering questions and giving directions. It seemed that if a decision needed to be made, all concerned were referred to this guy.

John was a nice looking fellow with a coiffed haircut and was wearing a nice shirt. The only thing that gave him away was the prison pants. As the meeting got underway, most of the sharing was from the inmates regarding their efforts to stay clean. Seems that contraband was easier to come by behind the prison walls than one would regularly assume. Their concerns were real, and the ones I heard really appeared sincere in their desire to remain clean and sober. Sometime later, John, the apparent leader, began his sharing opportunity. He said that keeping a good attitude was his main goal, but the fact that he was doing life in prison made it somewhat difficult. My thought was "Life in prison!" John had appeared to me to be a guy just trying to do his time, rehabilitate himself, and just get on with his life somewhere down the line. The life in prison thing baffled me, but the meeting resumed with me just moving ahead to hear what the rest of the guys had to say.

After the meeting and a little socializing, Jim showed me some of the beautiful leather book covers John had been making. I immediately said I wanted one and put in my order. Mine would have the AA emblem along with my initials carved into it. We said our goodbyes, and I told John I would be looking forward to receiving the book cover. While in the car exiting the prison grounds, I was still pondering John's situation, especially after he revealed that he was doing life in prison. Jim's answer to me when asked about John was in the form of a question. He asked me if I had ever heard of a Grand Ol' Opry star named Stringbean. I immediately knew where this was going, and knew it wasn't going to be pretty.

My grandma's conversation with my mom years before kept ringing in my ears. John Brown was the guy that murdered Stringbean and his wife. He had done the heinous crime in a drunken blackout. His cousin was convicted along with John for the murders. After a few surreal moments of being in shock, it was still absolutely hard to believe. The man, John, who I met inside the prison walls in no way seemed capable of such a deed.

A few years later, my friend Jim Boyd booked my band to do a concert inside the Lois DeBerry Special Needs Prison in

Nashville. Once again, John Brown was in charge. He was the guy rolling out the sound system, and basically just once again running the show. John was in charge of landscaping the prison grounds, and was still basically mentoring his fellow prisoners. Our show went well that night. My guys played well, and I had a great time playing for the captive audience in front of me. These guys were in for all sorts of crimes and serving all lengths of sentences from a few years to life. I was told later on that my show was the last one to be held in the prison. A new administration at the prison was put in place and shortly thereafter any and all such activities were discontinued. Evidently, the prisoners in attendance for our show that night had a great time and were still talking about it fifteen years later. Somewhere in between the TV show, City Confidential, featured Nashville, and honed in on the Stringbean and John Brown saga. It described the sequence of events and mentioned John Brown and his cousin, Doug Brown, along with showing photographs of each. Even though many years had passed, it was impossible for me to think that the person on TV was the same person I had met in the prison, or that he would be in any way capable of this crime.

Every few years, John Brown would come up for parole, and he would be continually rejected. I would stay in touch with Jim Boyd each time to follow the progress. It was hard to imagine and it seemed unlikely that parole would ever happen. Finally, after forty plus years in prison, Brown was granted parole in late 2014. His release made the national news, with TV news anchors actually questioning how he would hold up in the real world after his release as far as employment, etc. Since his release, and with the help of Jim Boyd, John has been employed doing landscape work and managing two car washes, and doing very well. His wife stayed with him through the whole forty year sentence, and she is still by his side. It was Boyd's commitment to John to help him after his release, since Brown had made sure that Jim was always safe during his many visits over the years into the prison. Jim Boyd said, "I vowed to give the next twenty-five years to John since he had given twenty-five years in helping me during my prison rehab efforts." Boyd added that John Brown remembered me from my performance at the prison, and from the book cover he had made for me. He suggested that I visit with John on my next trip to Nashville. I made it a point to do that.

In the summer of 2015, while attending a music convention in Nashville along with a booking at The Bluebird Café, I got to visit with John Brown and tell him the same story I'm telling you here. In my wanting to write this story, along with Jim Boyd's support, it was important that I sit down with John and tell him my intentions. He was interested in knowing what direction the story would take, which was totally understandable. While explaining this story in detail to him on how he touched my life as a result of the person he had become, I was determined that his story needed to be told. Telling my version of his story to John Brown may have been tougher on me than it was for him, since there were a couple of brief emotional interruptions for me during the conversation. John was totally on the same page with my desire to tell his story. He told me that, "My life is an open book. I have nothing to hide". If you have ever thought that a person cannot change, maybe this story might change your mind. It certainly did mine.

CAROLYNN MANN

Carolynn Mann is a world-renowned artist, who graduated from Hiwassee College, University of Tennessee, and Georgia State University, and has done post graduate work at Emory University and Middle Tennessee State University.

A native of East Tennessee, she lived and taught in various parts of the South before moving to the metropolitan Atlanta area in 1985.

Carolynn left her career as a full-time educator to immerse herself in her art, and she has studied with many internationally respected instructors. Her paintings appear in private, public, and commercial collections all over the world.

In 2015, she participated in her first Creative Writing Workshop at FoxTale Book Shoppe, allowing her to add writing to her creative endeavors.

Carolynn has two adult daughters, both of whom share her interests in dance and the arts.

The Mysterious Darkness

    The road rambled by the weathered sign, the gate did not meet the end post on the other side of the road. They had heard the stories from their friends and family. There was always curiosity and comments when they drove by the road. The off-road seemed abandon, it would be difficult to impossible for an automobile, maybe a four wheel drive could make it. It was gutted, rock strewn and seemed unused. She knew that there were stories from others who had walked up the road. They had heard the stories from their friends and family. Their Mom would comment occasionally of stories, one might say; 'those stories became adventures from their perspective'. Among the locals, the gates had sheltered many story. Mom talked of even dressing up and going to social events to the area, using familiar names from church or schools. Every one within a twelve mile radius knew a relative or a friend, who could relate the most interesting stories.

    All of this carried an interesting appeal! Their age and lack of adventures were a factor, and the fact, "it was there," might have been all the intrigue they needed. It was possible to walk the road. This walk required a great amount of energy, up the steep hillside grade. With some exploration, one could traverse the knob, which is more than a hill and less than a mountain, without walking the road. The car or truck could be left on another road and no curiosity would be aroused. There were several lesser known openings, without signs. No sign was visible to remind us there was no invitation, and no one was around; except this party of three.

Getting their jackets and stuffing the flashlight into their back pockets was their first direction. They left the old car, locked, and began the flat trail, dodging the undergrowth and began the hillside. She followed the two backs in front of her, very conscious of their speed. She watched where she was to place her feet. The trail appeared to be an animal trail, one that the deer might use for foraging and water, weaving among the trees and undergrowth. The boys quickness and speed soon gave her thought that their first endeavor was to leave her behind. Hustle! She would not miss this outing, nor would they lose her before getting up the hill.

She would have to admit she adored these boys, an older brother and the younger. Not that she would admit to them, even on a little finger dare. There had never been an "I love you." Yet, there were visible signs of respect, much teasing and inappropriate remarks. There was an unspoken pack sealed with genetics and honored when the occasion was necessary. It appeared the two boys had already decided what this Sunday afternoon would be about, and who had decided to include her was not unclear, or a random inclusion expecting her to want to do something else and not go. The "yes" came clear, quick, decisive, loud, with exclamation.

There had been some discussion about the Native Americans living in the area, artifacts found. It was rumored that the Indians had used the opening for shelter and meetings. She knew the delight of finding arrowheads, the flints with triangular shaped stones, flat on the sides, and the indentations on the broad side, the area where attachments were made to the willow limb. The willow was straight and strong, flying accurately. Feathers were attached to the end, adding balance and accuracy. True, it would be a prize to find arrowheads. Several friends had collections. Some boasted of the largest arrowhead, the best color, the smallest, the largest numbers, and on and on. There could be pottery shards as the Indian had also used the area for residency. She had decided that one of her efforts would go to finding evidence to support the Indians presence, possible smoke stains in the cave, abandon flints and stones that could have been used and left.

They were going underground by choice, in front of them was a hole about three feet in reckless diameter, surrounded by two cedars, scrub bushes and a canopy of hard woods overhead. Many oak and hickory trees with acorns, hickory nuts and dried leaves about two inches deep. There was a rustle with each step. They were surrounded by old growth, trees 18 inches in diameter. Coming from another directions, they might have missed the opening. It was obvious that the boys were well aware of the hole into the earth, and had been here before. It was a naturally made opening, not even the animal trails were near.

The truth included a rugged entrance, a hole and much darkness beyond. The sunlight shown bright above them, and the flash lights in their hands could not hold the excitement, the void or penitrate the darkness. To enter, one must sit and extend the legs downward, trusting that the body would move in the best direction to a mound of dirt. Also, would it be dry enough to allow purchase with their tennis shoes? Finding that toe hold that would allow them to move slowing down into the opening was questionable. With the slowness of their movement, their eyes were beginning to adjust to the darkness. Then came the daunting task, sliding down the mound, finding groves in the dirt to move to the floor. Somewhere, she might have thought, "how will I get out of here?" Only she did not remember any thought of that manner. Youth? Perhaps it was the unknown, maybe the darkness, or the reality of possibilities that could have created a fear. There were no signs relating unsafe, and from the limited experience of the teens, it all seemed possible. There were three of them, three flashlights, and a full Sunday afternoon for adventure and exploration.

Holding on to the ledge, with legs extended down, it became a slide, even the water washed notches could support the weight. Realizing that she had been given the "ladies first"; looking down into the dark, she gasped, "you go first!" Her confidence, femininity, grace and athletic form would mount the confidence; as she crawled out and extending her arm and hand, she directed for one of the boys to precede her. Standing her ground with determination, she related, "You first!" with her eyebrows lifted and firm. Certain that once he was inside, her sense of fear would be abated.

She had traveled with her brothers before, she was known throughout the neighborhood as a "tom boy", except she did not feel masculine. Sure she could match wits with the guys, her DNA was the same as the boys. There was a bond among the three, however, the boys were know to test her with pranks, to see her bravery or lack there of. All found humor in some of the pranks and comments.

So the entrance was made, all had managed the semi free fall, advancing down the rise of dirt with little distress. The floor of the cave where they were was not level, and the conversation began, "Where?" "What do we do know?" "Now?" The lights go out!

Darkness has no meaning until one is in a cave. Even when the iris's have adjusted, not even the person beside you, is visible, their arm brushed her arm. Waiting and wanting to create that image, her mind does not work. Her creative mind senses fear of the unknown, not visions of the world just left. The blackness initiates more fear of the dark, permeating the body totally, and she stood in silence.

Sounds became audible, even from the darkness, perhaps her mind was searching for a touch of reality. The sounds amplify. A drip, a breath, a swosh of the mouth, and the mind begins the search for images, focusing on the direction, and she screams, "Turn the lights back on!"

There was a path, cut trough the red clay with the years of past travel, it was uneven, and they needed to watch and be aware of where the feet will land. Step downs are almost invisible unless they were focusing directly on the trail and the light was in that direction. They paused to watch the light play across the ceiling, now directly above. The walls were of muted neutral tones reflecting variations of sandstone shapes. Ahead, the trail looks like it ended, going into a wall, and arriving there, the opening between two walls allowed them to slip through sideway.

The three spend time exploring, following the trail, which sometimes extends to the left and a wall, or to the right, all unknown. The man made patterns are the dug out paths for walking. Occasionally, something familiar appears, and she states, "We have been here before." They then move into another direction, and one of the boys asks, "Are we lost?"

Each comment was spaced and repeated several times at different locations. There is a faint smell of smoke, a scent, and when she ask the others, they bravely noted, "No, I did not smell anything. Did you?"

From the different spaces, they could hear their voices reflecting back. In the large rooms, they would force the echos, sometimes softly and other times with a loud shouts. The echo rebounded through the stillness.

There was moisture, drops of water at certain places, creating some of the earths delicate formations. The shapes were stalactites and stalagmites, depending on their source, the ceiling or the earth. The chemicals, metals and elements of the earth blending with the compounds in the air and water, producing these visuals. Sometimes the drops of water could be heard, a splash, splink or splunk depending on the size of the drop. In the darkness, she could not always discern the location. Even in this alien space of darkness, most of the sounds could be identified. The darkness was ever present, the flashlights would penetrate the darkness in a cone shape a few feet ahead with a radius of 8 to 10 feet.

The faint memory came to her from their Mom's comment, she had been dancing here. Her thoughts became a question, "But, Mom, how could you have gone dancing there?" Realizing how dark it was.

The memory of her answer came, "When I was young, before children, everyone would gather there. A band and music, and there was electrial lighting. We would take fancy shoes, and dance the hours away." She realized now, how difficult that must have been.

Before her, the flash lights revealed a broad expanse of boards. About 40'x60', counting her strides with placement of the brothers and their lights at opposite ends. Around the flooring, the soil was still irregular, smooth and somewhat level. At one end was a separate section, space maybe for a small 3 man band, banjo, fiddle, and base.

"Wow!" she said loudly. Apparently the brothers were

aware of the dance floor and the structure. The room was the largest and the most level that they had been in. The walls were vast, ceiling tall and jagged with shapes. Their lights tunnelled across to the walls; all lights were needed to be focused to see the parts of the ceiling. She heard the question, "Who do you think carried all these 2x4's down, and how many trips to get everything needed here?"

She said, "O, this would be a great place to dance, could you sing?" Both turned off their flashlights and stood silently, letting the darkness absorb the space into her narrow shaft of light.

From the darkness, he carefully constructed his next sentence, as if there was someone else in the room; a deeper, a slower Southern draw, "I remember Pa talking about cock fights, here."

The younger brother picked up on the charade, with a squeky voice, noted, "This would be an easy place to disappear and be off the community radar. If anyone wanted to do something illegal, here is the place."

The elder said, "Moonshine!" in the false base voice as if another.

"Enough. Enough talking!" she related in her natural voice, there might have been a shiver with the sounds. She was shaping her confidence back. She was ready to move on, and with walking, she paid attention to the passage way. She was focusing on keeping her mind away from conceived dangers. After all, they were the only humans in this cave today. Sometimes, it was difficult to know what was real and what they were exaggerating.

They came upon red embers of a still warm fire, a chamber they had just passed through about a couple of hours ago. There was no fire then. Now, it was obvious that a fire had been lite. There came many speculative comments, "Someone else is here. Who? Where?"

"Do they mean harm?", another asked.

"Will they try to harm us?"

"How many people?"

"Where did they go?"

She would have admitted the alarm bells sounded in her

mind. No one asked. And if the guys were honest, they too might have said, "this situation does not have the ring of safety!"

"Let's look around and check the area", was the next comment. They began to walk, using the lights to illuminate the sides.

About 100 yards around one of the invisible crevices, they found indentations in the clay. Investigating, all three decided it was where hips were placed, as if seated, one on the right side, two on the left.

They looked to each others for answers and speculation. Faces ghostly lit by the lights at the end of each arm. There was no comment. Each began searching the room, and then the spaces where individuals had sat. To one side of the hip print was a droplet, a circle of moisture. They automatically looked at each other as if drawn by a magnet. No one wanted to touch it, nor comment. The circle was about two inch oval, dark, spaced close to the butt prints. No questions, only silence.

The eldest moved a hand in the opposite direction they had come, circling without a word, each of the three, and pointed to the direction of the prints. It was the encouragment that we needed, all three together. There was silence, they could not hear any sounds. They stopped at another print about 20 feet beyond, more moisture, and the word stated as a question, "Blood?"

She was hesitant, her feeling of confidence had bleedinto fear and insecurity. She reasoned she could see nothing. There were no human sounds of walking, talking, breathing, and yet there were other people inside the cave, and there was an equal number, if the butt prints were represntative of everyone, and no one standing while others rested. There could be more of them than the three family members of youth. Not sure how far ahead of the family, and the prints looked like adults, large and expansive. Why were they here?

They moved quietly, no sounds, moving the lights to the right and the left, looking for anything that was out of the ordinary. Another print, only one now, and the dark drops began to be every 3 to 6 feet, without a print. Drop, drop,

drop, spot, drops.

They paused, caught their breath, and in a whisper, asked questions.

"Who could this be?"

"How many people are there?"

"Where are they going"

"What are those drops? Blood?"

"What are we going to do? How are we getting out of here?"

The questions were asked so quickly and quietly, neither had time to answer. Realizing that staying inside was not a viable option. No one knew where the kids were, there would be no parental alarm until after dark. They were trusted to do what was right and the knowledge that they could take care of each other. "They had each others back!" was their usual comment. They had never been in a situation that could be this dangerous and unsafe.

She lifted her hand for quiet. The eldest flashed a thumb with the sofest voice, "Out." It was the direction of the spots, as the alarms sounded confirming her fear inside her head. Heading out was a choice of safety or possible harm. This was the puzzle created that neither of them said.

The steps became quicker and softer, almost soundless. There were no voices, if some one wanted to say something, it was silent with a gesture of the arm and hand. Motions were the communications, a flat hand against a shoulder startled her, the Younger paused. They stopped, he had his finger to his lips and then moved it to his ear. Alarmed, the lights go out quickly, and they listened, not even the labored breath from their bodies making a sound.

Their pause seemed like minutes, half an hour. The Eldest, touched, and the lights came on as they continued. More spots of moisture, about the same frequency, every 6 feet, and they were beginning to be smaller in size. They were on high alert, watching for lights moving ahead, listening for foot steps, breathing, pantleg swishing, anything to confirm the individuals were close. As she let out the air in her lungs, searching for breath of safety, hoping for no sounds or light affirming others in the distance.

JULIE COUSE

Julie Couse began writing letters to an adult friend of the family when she was eight years old. The appreciation and praise she received prompted her to write letters to other people. Later, as a teen, she collaborated with her younger brother on a fantasy story entitled, "The Spinach Lasagna that Ate Kings Dominion" (an amusement park in Virginia), illustrating to her how much fun writing can be.

In 2012, Julie took her first Writing Class at FoxTale. For a class in 2015, she wrote "The Artist's Rap" (the piece included in this Anthology), for which she earned high praise from her classmates. It represented a "stretch" from her usual non-fiction and poetry, and she continues to expand her writing horizons by dabbling in novel-writing for NaNoWriMo each November.

Julie's career includes nursing assistant, accounting & loss prevention at a newspaper, university student housing office, and a variety of positions in the computer/technology industry. Currently, she works in quality assurance for an ethics & compliance hotline reporting service, and is aspiring to write non-fiction pieces covering medical or science topics. She holds a B.S. in Psychology from Virginia Commonwealth University.

In 2009, Julie lost her husband, Rick, to whom she was married for 18 years. Her family includes her mother, sister, and two brothers (one in New York, one in Virginia), and she cherishes her time with her nieces and nephews.

The Artist's Rap

Now here I go I'm on the way of the artist
I'm tellin' you I think it's the smartest
thing I've ever done.
It's so much fun.

I will tell you that the hardest
part is thinking of the things I missed when I was young
things I wasn't doin'
'cause I was too into
thinking that I could not and I should not.
That's not so hot
But I forgot
Or never knew that yes I could oh yes I should
and yes I would and yes it's good.
But now I know
I'm good to go
Let's start the show
I'm sayin', yo,
I am the artist
I'll go the farthest
You'll see my best and I won't rest until I know
I make my art straight from the heart and here's the part
I'm ready to shout
Let my artist out!
It's all about
Stopping the block
before you've got to stop the clock.

It's time to do what makes us joyous
Do not annoy us with a quest for perfection
It's not the best. It's deception

telling us we can't be good enough.
Forget that stuff!
Let's pay attention
and show up every day so we can play
with creativity and go the artist's way.

ABOUT THE EDITOR

Beth Hermes began facilitating writing workshops and classes at FoxTale Book Shoppe in 2009, and has helped inspire more than 150 writers over the last six years.

In 2014, the Shoppe added Beth's monthly Critique Workshops and Creative Writing Boot Camps to the list of offerings, which allowed aspiring writers with full schedules to pursue their craft.

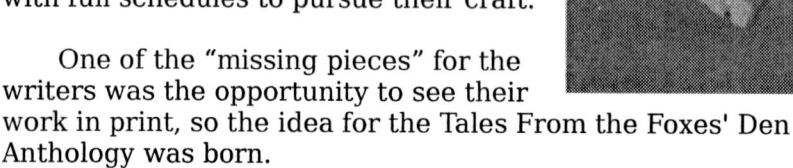

One of the "missing pieces" for the writers was the opportunity to see their work in print, so the idea for the Tales From the Foxes' Den Anthology was born.

A writer herself for more than 30 years, Beth began her career in journalism, writing for newspapers and magazines. She parlayed her skills into marketing for a non-profit organization and the real estate industry, and began offering her services as a freelance writer to individuals and small businesses in 2008.

Beth is the author of a spiritual/fantasy series, "The Lightbearers Books," and is currently working on a memoir.

A graduate of Auburn University's School of Journalism, Beth resides in Canton, Georgia, with her husband, Craig, son, Benjamin, several rescue dogs, a horse, and a turtle. Their daughter, Abigail, is a professional artist.

WRITING WORKSHOPS AT FOXTALE BOOK SHOPPE

FoxTale Book Shoppe hosts numerous writing workshops and workshop series throughout each year.

Call 770-516-9989, or check our upcoming workshop schedule by visiting our website: www.foxtalebookshoppe.com/writers/

Better yet, sign up for our email newsletter, where you will learn about upcoming writing classes, plus news about authors, new releases, children's events, and more!